Math Builder

Jessika Sobanski

LEARNINGEXPRESS

New York

Library of Congress Caloging-in-Publication Data:
Sobanski, Jessika.
    Math builder / by Jessika Sobanski.—1st ed.
        p. cm.
    ISBN 1-57685-390-X
    1. Mathematics—Problems, exercises, etc. 2. Mathematics—Study and teaching
(Elementary) I. Title.

    QA43 .S663 2001
    510'.76—dc21

                                                        2001046189

Printed in the United States of America
9 8 7 6 5 4 3 2
First Edition

ISBN 1-57685-390-X

For more information or to place an order, contact LearningExpress at:
    55 Broadway
    8th Floor
    New York, NY 10006

Or visit us at:
www.learnatest.com

CONTENTS

INTRODUCTION

Welcome to *Math Builder*. This book represents a progression of sets of math questions that build math skills. The beginning sets of each section are the most basic, and successive sets get more and more complex. Thus, by design, this book is perfect for anybody seeking to attain better math skills. In addition, if you are studying for a particular test, you can use the following chart to quickly pinpoint the sets that will best suit your needs. Information for each test follows the chart. It is important to note that if the chart indicates a **Warm Up** or **Test Prep** set that seems too hard for you, you should just drop down to a lower-level set and work your way up.

Test:	COOP	HSPT	GED	ASVAB	SAT*/PSAT*	College Entrance
Misc. Math	*Warm Up:* Set 3 *Test Prep:* Set 4 Set 5 Set 6	*Test Prep:* Set 2 Set 3 Set 4 Set 5	*Test Prep:* Set 2 Set 4 Set 5 Set 6	*Test Prep:* Set 1 Set 2 Set 3 Set 4 Set 5	*Warm Up:* Set 3 *Test Prep:* Set 4 Set 5 Set 6	*Test Prep:* Set 2 Set 3 Set 4 Set 5 Set 6
Fractions	*Warm Up:* Set 7 Set 8 *Test Prep:* Set 9 Set 10 Set 11	*Test Prep:* Set 7 Set 8 Set 9 Set 10 Set 11	*Warm Up:* Set 7 Set 8 *Test Prep:* Set 9 Set 10 Set 11	*Test Prep:* Set 8 Set 9 Set 10 Set 11	*Test Prep:* Set 9 Set 10 Set 11	*Warm Up:* Set 7 *Test Prep:* Set 8 Set 9 Set 10 Set 11
Decimals	*Warm Up:* Set 12 Set 13 Set 14 Set 16 *Test Prep:* Set 15 Set 17	*Test Prep:* Set 12 Set 13 Set 14 Set 16	*Warm Up:* Set 12 Set 13 Set 14 Set 16 *Test Prep:* Set 15 Set 17	*Warm Up:* Set 12 Set 13 Set 14 *Test Prep:* Set 16	*Warm Up:* Set 16 *Test Prep:* Set 17	*Test Prep:* Set 12 Set 13 Set 14 Set 15 Set 16 Set 17

Test:	COOP	HSPT	GED	ASVAB	SAT*/PSAT*	College Entrance
Percents	*Warm Up:* Set 18 Set 19 *Test Prep:* Set 20 Set 21 Set 23	*Test Prep:* Set 18 Set 19 Set 21 Set 22 Set 23	*Test Prep:* Set 20 Set 21 Set 22 Set 23	*Test Prep:* Set 18 Set 19 Set 21 Set 22 Set 23	*Warm Up:* Set 18 Set 19 *Test Prep:* Set 20 Set 21 Set 22 Set 23	*Test Prep:* Set 18 Set 19 Set 20 Set 21 Set 22 Set 23
Algebra	*Warm Up:* Set 24 *Test Prep:* Set 25 Set 26 Set 27 Set 28	*Test Prep:* Set 24 Set 26 Set 27 Set 28	*Warm Up:* Set 24 *Test Prep:* Set 25 Set 26 Set 27 Set 28 Set 29 Set 30	*Test Prep:* Set 24 Set 26 Set 27 Set 28	*Warm Up:* Set 24 Set 25 Set 26 *Test Prep:* Set 27 Set 28 Set 29 Set 30	*Test Prep:* Set 24 Set 25 Set 26 Set 27 Set 28 Set 29 Set 30
Geometry	*Warm Up:* Set 31 *Test Prep:* Set 32 Set 33 Set 34 Set 35	*Warm Up:* Set 31 *Test Prep:* Set 32 Set 33 Set 35	*Test Prep:* Set 33 Set 34 Set 35 Set 36 Set 37	*Test Prep:* Set 31 Set 33 Set 34 Set 35	*Test Prep:* Set 33 Set 34 Set 35 Set 38	*Test Prep:* Set 31 Set 32 Set 33 Set 34 Set 35 Set 36 Set 37 Set 38

*Read the following important information regarding the levels of SAT questions addressed in this book.

COOP

The **Mathematics Concepts and Applications** section of the COOP test assesses your basic math skills, your understanding of mathematic principles and rules, and your problem solving abilities. There is a strong focus on assessing your ability to set up mathematical calculations instead of actually solving the problems. In addition, you are expected to interpret data from pie charts, tables, and diagrams in order to compute your answers. The **Test Prep** sets listed on pages vi and vii are simulations of actual COOP questions, but practicing with the **Warm Up** questions is highly recommended. These questions may not be *exactly* like the ones you'll see on your COOP exam, but the concepts and skills addressed are very important for you to know.

HSPT

The **Mathematics** section of the HSPT test is designed to test your knowledge of math concepts and problem solving. The **Test Prep** sets listed above are simulations of actual HSPT questions. Also, practicing with the **Warm Up** questions is highly recommended. These questions may not be *exactly* like the ones you'll see on your real exam, but the concepts and skills addressed are very important for you to review.

GED

People from many different walks of life decide to take the GED. You may be a teenager who decided to leave high school to go to work and are determined to get your GED on your own. You may be an adult who has always wanted to take this test. In any case, using this book is ideal for you, no matter where you are in your studies or your life. First try out the guidelines in the chart above. Start with the **Warm Up** sets. If these seem too unfamiliar, or difficult, go back to the first set of the section and build your way up. Eventually, you will be able to complete the **Test Prep** sets. These questions are just like the ones you will see on test day. Don't skip the **Warm Up** questions! These questions may not be *exactly* like the ones you'll see on your real exam, but the concepts and skills addressed are very important for you to review.

The math section of the GED starts off with a full page of conversions. For example: 1 foot = 12 inches, 1 hour = 60 minutes, and so forth. Don't forget about this reference page when you take the test! As you complete the practice sets, the pertinent information is provided with the question itself. On the day of your test, you will look it up for yourself.

ASVAB

All three math sections on the ASVAB are covered in this book:

- Arithmetic Reasoning
- Numerical Operations
- Mathematics Knowledge

It is advised that you adhere to the **Warm Up** sets and **Test Prep** sets outlined in the chart on pages vi and vii. Set 1 correlates to the **Numerical Operations** part of the ASVAB. It is a speed and accuracy drill, and is the easiest math you will see on the exam. The math problems that you'll calculate in the **Arithmetic Reasoning** section are word problems that test your understanding of: *whole numbers, fractions, decimals, money, ratios, proportions, percent, interest, geometry, and measurement.* The **Mathematics Knowledge** section tests your understanding of concepts and principles involving: *number theory, numeration, algebraic operations and equations, geometry and measurement, and probability.* As you can see there is an overlap in content on these two sections. Just know that if you run through all of the **Warm Up** and **Test Prep** sets outlined in the chart, you will be ready for all three math sections on the ASVAB.

SAT AND PSAT

The SAT and PSAT designate the difficulty of the questions based on a level from 1–5. Level 1 questions are the easiest, and Level 5 questions are the hardest. There are about six Level 5 questions on all of the math sections combined. It is possible to score over 700 (out of 800) on the math portion of the SAT without even answering these Level 5 questions. That is why you shouldn't be alarmed to find out that this book *does not* cover Level 5 questions. The levels covered are Levels 1–Level 4. It is in your best interest to get your hands on old SATs, so you can see the particular format that the SAT uses in testing your math skills (multiple choice, quantitative comparison, gridded response), and to view all of the subject matter. In this book, we concentrate on the four common SAT student pitfalls:

- Percents (including percent increase and decrease)
- Algebra
- Ratios
- Geometry

Every math section on the SAT starts with reference information. Make sure you take a peek at their formulas when you get stuck. As you work through the sets here, the relevant information is provided along with the question itself. For example, if it is a 30°–60°–90° tri-

angle question, we give you a 30°–60°–90° triangle. Also, good news: you are allowed to use a calculator on the SAT. And the bad news: there is a guessing penalty. You will get $\frac{1}{4} - \frac{1}{3}$ of a point deducted from your raw score for every wrong answer. Try to narrow your choices down before guessing. If you have no clue, leave it blank. (The "over 700" score mentioned above was for somebody leaving all six Level 5 questions *blank* and getting the remaining 54 questions right!)

COLLEGE ENTRANCE

The whole notion behind assessing your abilities as you enter a community or private college is to place you in an appropriate level math class. Most students do not wish to be assigned to a class that does not count as credit earned toward their degree. Therefore, using this book will build your skills so that you can test your way into a class that counts. Practically all of the sets in this book are appropriate for you, because you can always place higher. Ask the college you plan to attend for a sample test to really hone in on the sets that suit your needs.

OTHER TESTS

If you are preparing for a test other than the ones mentioned above, try to get your hands on a sample copy of the test. You can then use that test, along with this book, to build your way up to the level you need. Some sample tests do *not* come with detailed, easy to understand explanations of the topics presented. This book explains the most basic form of a question and then builds upon that knowledge with successive sets.

S·E·C·T·I·O·N
MISCELLANEOUS MATH

1

Miscellaneous Math consists of an array of math topics including: arithmetic, math concepts and principles, math terminology, unit conversions, exponents, radicals, proportions, ratios, probability, sequences, mean, median, mode, and chart interpretation. A lot of these same topics will be revisited in future sections. Here, they are presented at the most basic level, without fractions or decimals. You may have decided on a "game plan" from the introductory chapter as far as which sets are appropriate when preparing for a particular test. It is wise to follow the recommendations outlined in the chart, because although the general order of sets is from easy to more difficult, the content of the sets varies, and you need to be sure to expose yourself to all the different types of questions that you will see. Start building your math proficiency with these six sets.

SET 1: SPEED AND ACCURACY DRILL (3 MINUTES)

1. $45 \div 9 =$
- a. 4
- b. 5
- c. 6
- d. 7

2. $7 \times 8 =$
- a. 36
- b. 48
- c. 56
- d. 60

3. $12 + 5 =$
- a. 17
- b. 18
- c. 19
- d. 20

4. $84 \div 7 =$
- a. 11
- b. 12
- c. 77
- d. 91

5. $19 - 8 =$
- a. 11
- b. 12
- c. 13
- d. 14

6. $45 \div 3 =$
- a. 42
- b. 48
- c. 13
- d. 15

7. $9 + 4 =$
- a. 36
- b. 16
- c. 13
- d. 5

8. $20 - 7 =$
- a. 14
- b. 13
- c. 12
- d. 11

9. $4 \times 8 =$
- a. 12
- b. 24
- c. 28
- d. 32

10. $18 + 6 =$
- a. 12
- b. 32
- c. 24
- d. 26

11. $56 \div 8 =$
- a. 6
- b. 7
- c. 8
- d. 9

12. $15 - 8 =$
- a. 7
- b. 8
- c. 9
- d. 23

13. $55 \div 11 =$
- a. 44
- b. 66
- c. 6
- d. 5

14. $6 + 9 =$
   a. 14
   b. 15
   c. 16
   d. 17

15. $7 \times 12 =$
   a. 72
   b. 63
   c. 84
   d. 96

16. $4 + 11 =$
   a. 16
   b. 15
   c. 13
   d. 12

17. $54 \div 6 =$
   a. 6
   b. 7
   c. 8
   d. 9

18. $34 - 7 =$
   a. 27
   b. 26
   c. 25
   d. 24

19. $18 \div 6 =$
   a. 24
   b. 12
   c. 3
   d. 4

20. $13 + 8 =$
   a. 25
   b. 23
   c. 22
   d. 21

21. $52 - 8 =$
   a. 44
   b. 46
   c. 36
   d. 34

22. $10 \times 20 =$
   a. 30
   b. 20
   c. 200
   d. 120

23. $101 + 102 =$
   a. 212
   b. 221
   c. 203
   d. 230

24. $96 \div 3 =$
   a. 32
   b. 33
   c. 23
   d. 22

25. $35 \div 5 =$
   a. 6
   b. 40
   c. 8
   d. 7

26. $64 \div 4 =$
   a. 24
   b. 18
   c. 17
   d. 16

27. $5 \times 12 =$
   a. 55
   b. 60
   c. 65
   d. 70

28. $7 + 16 =$
a. 23
b. 22
c. 21
d. 20

29. $48 \div 6 =$
a. 6
b. 7
c. 8
d. 9

30. $21 - 7 =$
a. 13
b. 14
c. 12
d. 11

31. $24 \div 3 =$
a. 8
b. 6
c. 5
d. 4

32. $22 + 24 =$
a. 40
b. 42
c. 44
d. 46

33. $54 - 20 =$
a. 36
b. 34
c. 32
d. 26

34. $10 \times 7 =$
a. 62
b. 67
c. 70
d. 77

35. $29 + 9 =$
a. 34
b. 36
c. 38
d. 39

36. $39 \div 13 =$
a. 6
b. 5
c. 4
d. 3

37. $42 - 6 =$
a. 36
b. 38
c. 46
d. 48

38. $108 \div 9 =$
a. 10
b. 11
c. 12
d. 13

39. $15 + 17 =$
a. 31
b. 32
c. 33
d. 34

40. $6 \times 12 =$
a. 54
b. 68
c. 72
d. 80

41. $53 + 56 =$
a. 103
b. 105
c. 107
d. 109

42. $132 \div 12 =$
   a. 11
   b. 12
   c. 13
   d. 14

43. $100 - 25 =$
   a. 70
   b. 75
   c. 82
   d. 85

44. $48 \div 16 =$
   a. 5
   b. 4
   c. 3
   d. 6

45. $210 + 17 =$
   a. 227
   b. 207
   c. 210
   d. 220

46. $45 - 4 =$
   a. 42
   b. 41
   c. 40
   d. 39

47. $17 \times 3 =$
   a. 39
   b. 41
   c. 43
   d. 51

48. $8 + 5 =$
   a. 9
   b. 12
   c. 13
   d. 14

49. $58 \div 2 =$
   a. 29
   b. 28
   c. 34
   d. 32

50. $92 \div 4 =$
   a. 36
   b. 23
   c. 26
   d. 32

SET 2

51. 4! is equivalent to:
   a. 4×4
   b. $4 \times 3 \times 2 \times 1$
   c. $4 \times 4 \times 4 \times 4$
   d. $4 \times 3 \times 2 \times 1 \times 0$

52. $(-5)(-3)(2) - |-20|$
   a. 50
   b. 40
   c. 20
   d. 10

53. $\sqrt{72} + \sqrt{200} =$
   a. $16\sqrt{2}$
   b. $\sqrt{272}$
   c. $4\sqrt{2}$
   d. $6\sqrt{3}$

54. $121 - 2(11 - 8)^3 =$
   a. 107
   b. 103
   c. 67
   d. -95

55. Which of the following is divisible by 7 and 5?
- a. 28
- b. 40
- c. 77
- d. 105

56. 17,822 can also be represented as
- a. 1000 + 700 + 80 + 2
- b. 10000 + 7000 + 200 + 80 + 2
- c. 10000 + 7000 + 800 + 2
- d. 10000 + 7000 + 800 + 20 + 2

57. Which set represents 4 consecutive even numbers whose sum is 44?
- a. {7, 9, 11, 17}
- b. {4, 6, 8, 10}
- c. {8, 10, 12, 14}
- d. none of the above

58. 12^3 is equal to
- a. $12 \div 3$
- b. $12 \cdot 12 \cdot 12$
- c. 12×12
- d. $12 \times 11 \times 10 \times 9 \times 8 \times 7 \times 6 \times 5 \times 4 \times 3 \times 2 \times 1$

59. $(12 \times 5) - 8 =$
- a. −36
- b. 42
- c. 52
- d. 68

60. $\sqrt{125}$ is equivalent to
- a. 5
- b. $5\sqrt{5}$
- c. $5\sqrt{25}$
- d. $25\sqrt{5}$

61. 5^3 is equal to
- a. 15
- b. 25
- c. 75
- d. 125

62. $3\sqrt{32}$ can also be written as
- a. $3\sqrt{16 \cdot 2}$
- b. $3\sqrt{4 \cdot 2}$
- c. $3 \cdot 2\sqrt{2}$
- d. $6\sqrt{2}$

63. $\sqrt{1151}$ to the nearest tenth is
- a. 29.7
- b. 33.9
- c. 35.8
- d. 37.2

64. $13 \times 13 \times 13 \times 13 \times 13$ is equivalent to
- a. 13!
- b. $13^2 + 13^3$
- c. 13^5
- d. 13^{-5}

65. $\sqrt[3]{125}$ is equal to
- a. −5
- b. −11
- c. 11
- d. 5

66. $\sqrt{\frac{1}{64}}$ is equivalent to
- a. 8
- b. $\frac{1}{8}$
- c. 4
- d. $\frac{1}{4}$

67. $(-2)^3 + (-3)^2 =$
- a. 35
- b. 19
- c. 17
- d. 1

68. $\sqrt{51}$ when rounded to the nearest tenth is equivalent to
 a. 6.5
 b. 6.8
 c. 7.1
 d. 8.2

69. 25^2 is how much greater than 21^2?
 a. 184
 b. 40
 c. 18
 d. 4

70. $|-16 \times -2 + 5 \times 8| =$
 a. 384
 b. 8
 c. 608
 d. 72

SET 3

71. Which of the following is divisible by 8 and 6?
 a. 16
 b. 24
 c. 32
 d. 38

72. 13,450 can be also represented as
 a. $1,000 + 300 + 40 + 5$
 b. $10,000 + 4,000 + 300 + 50$
 c. $10,000 + 3,000 + 400 + 50$
 d. $10,000 + 5,000 + 400 + 30$

73. Which set represents 4 consecutive odd numbers whose sum is 24?
 a. {3, 5, 7, 9}
 b. {4, 6, 8, 10}
 c. {3, 6, 7, 8}
 d. none of the above

74. What is another way to write 6^3?
 a. 6×6
 b. $6 \times 6 \times 6 \times 6$
 c. $6 \times 5 \times 4 \times 3 \times 2 \times 1$
 d. 36×6

75. Which value is equal to the square root of 64?
 a. $\sqrt[3]{64}$
 b. $4\sqrt{4}$
 c. $4\sqrt{2}$
 d. 8^2

76. The greatest common factor of 56 and 64 is
 a. 4
 b. 6
 c. 8
 d. 9

77. Choose the expression that corresponds with the following statement: *The quotient of nine divided by three is decreased by one.*
 a. $9 \div 3 - 1$
 b. $9 \div (3 - 1)$
 c. $1 - 9 \div 3$
 d. $(1 - 9) \div 3$

78. When the product of 250 and 213 is rounded to the nearest hundred, the solution is
 a. 40,000
 b. 53,200
 c. 53,250
 d. 53,300

79. Which answer choice represents factors that 56 and 96 have in common?
 a. 1, 14, 8
 b. 2, 8, 12
 c. 3, 12, 16
 d. none of the above

80. $(-6) + 13 =$
a. -7
b. 7
c. 19
d. -19

81. $(-9)^2 =$
a. -81
b. -18
c. 81
d. 18

82. $(-2)^5 =$
a. 16
b. -16
c. 32
d. -32

83. $3 \times 3 \times 3 \times 3 \times 3$ can be written as
a. 3!
b. 3^6
c. 3^5
d. 81

84. What is the square root of 121?
a. 7
b. 10.3
c. 11
d. 13

85. Which number sentence is true?
a. 8 oz. > 12 oz.
b. 7 oz. < 9 oz.
c. 9 oz. > 12 oz.
d. 8 oz. > 9 oz.

86. Which of the following represents twenty-three thousand, five hundred and seventeen?
a. 235,017
b. 23,317
c. 23,517
d. 2,317

87. $13^3 =$
a. 39
b. 169
c. 297
d. 2197

88. $(-8) \times (-5) =$
a. -45
b. -40
c. 40
d. 45

89. Eleven thousand, two hundred and fifty-seven is expressed mathematically as
a. 11,257
b. 1257
c. 101,257
d. 110,257

90. Which number sentence is true?
a. $7 \text{ cm} + 5 \text{ cm} > 4 \text{ cm} + 8 \text{ cm}$
b. $4 \text{ cm} + 8 \text{ cm} \geq 7 \text{ cm} + 5 \text{ cm}$
c. $6 \text{ cm} + 4 \text{ cm} < 12 \text{ cm} - 6 \text{ cm}$
d. $12 \text{ cm} - 6 \text{ cm} \geq 6 \text{ cm} + 4 \text{ cm}$

SET 4

91. Fill in the missing term in the following sequence: 31 23 17 13 ___
   a. 12
   b. 11
   c. 7
   d. 5

92. The ratio of 20 to 50 can be represented by
   a. 50:20
   b. 1:2
   c. 2:1
   d. 2:5

93. The quiz scores for 7 students are listed below:
   12 10 14 8 7 3 13
   What is the median score?
   a. 12
   b. 10
   c. 8
   d. 7

94. A heating bill of $540 is to be paid equally by six housemates. How much will each person pay?
   a. $90
   b. $80
   c. $70
   d. $60

95. Which statement is true regarding the following numbers: 12 14 15 19 20 22
   a. The average is greater than the median.
   b. The median is greater than the mean.
   c. The mean equals the median.
   d. The mean is greater than the average.

96. What is the mode of the following numbers?
   35 52 17 23 51 52 18 32
   a. 52
   b. 35
   c. 33.5
   d. 18

97. Cassie bought five CDs. The average price per CD came out to $13. If she knows that three CDs cost $12, and the fourth cost $15, what was the price of the fifth CD?
   a. $12
   b. $13
   c. $14
   d. $15

98. Per 1,000,000 molecules of air there are 78,083 molecules of nitrogen, 20,945 molecules of oxygen, and 35 molecules of carbon dioxide. What is the ratio of carbon dioxide to oxygen?
   a. 20,945:35
   b. 35:78,083
   c. 7:4189
   d. 945:8,083

99. Joe bought a new car. $1600 was deducted from the selling price for trading in his old car, and he will pay off the remainder in equal monthly installments over the course of 5 years. If the total cost for the car is $14,200, how much is Joe's monthly payment?
   a. $236
   b. $234
   c. $224
   d. $210

100. What number is missing from this sequence?

11 28 ___ 62 79

a. 30

b. 45

c. 48

d. 51

101. As a promotion, a record company will hand out random cassettes to a crowd. If the company brought along 300 rap cassettes, 500 hard rock cassettes, 200 easy listening cassettes, and 400 country cassettes, what is the probability that a given person will get an easy listening cassette?

a. $\frac{1}{8}$

b. $\frac{1}{7}$

c. $\frac{1}{6}$

d. $\frac{1}{5}$

102. A link light steadily blinks two times every three seconds. How many times will it blink in ten minutes?

a. $6\frac{2}{3}$

b. 40

c. 66

d. 400

103. The square root of 35 is

a. between 6 and 7.

b. between 5 and 6.

c. between 4 and 5.

d. between 3 and 4.

104. A particle that is 4×10^4 mm is how much larger than a particle that is 2×10^2 mm?

a. It is twice as large.

b. It is 20 times as large.

c. It is 200 times as large.

d. It is $\frac{1}{2}$ as large.

105. If eight people are needed to manage two power plants, which expression represents the number of people needed to manage 30 power plants?

a. $8 \times 30 \div 2$

b. $8 \times 2 \div 30$

c. $2 \times 30 \div 8$

d. none of the above

SET 5

106. If a train car can fit 54 people, which expression below represents the number of train cars necessary to carry 324 people?

a. 54×324

b. $324 \div 54$

c. $324 - 54$

d. none of the above

107. A carbon monoxide detector reads 50 parts per million (ppm) at 9 A.M. and 1350 ppm at 12 noon. This most nearly indicates that the concentration of carbon monoxide

a. quadrupled every hour.

b. tripled every hour.

c. doubled every hour.

d. remained constant.

108. A gallon of wiper fluid costs 95 cents. How many dollars will 3 gallons cost?

a. $285

b. $270

c. $2.85

d. $2.70

109. A six-sided die with sides numbered 1 through 6 is rolled. What is the probability that the number rolled is a multiple of 3?

   a. $\frac{1}{3}$

   b. $\frac{1}{6}$

   c. $\frac{2}{3}$

   d. $\frac{3}{6}$

110. Studies show that a lion's roar can be heard five miles away. It would therefore be correct to state that a lion's roar can be heard from how many inches away?

   a. 316.8 inches

   b. 600 inches

   c. 26,400 inches

   d. 316,800 inches

111. Darren's band played for 1 hour and 35 minutes. Ray's band played for 1 hour and 40 minutes. When combined, the two performances lasted how long?

   a. 5 min.

   b. 1 hr. 15 min.

   c. 2 hr. 75 min.

   d. 3 hr. 15 min.

112. Andy combines 12 ounces of new grain with 8 ounces of old grain inside a container. How much grain is inside the container?

   a. 2 lb. 4 oz.

   b. 20 lbs.

   c. 1 lb. 4 oz.

   d. 16 lbs.

113. Dan left at 8:35 A.M. and returned at 1:13 P.M. How much time elapsed while he was gone?

   a. 4 hr. 38 min.

   b. 5 hr. 38 min.

   c. 4 hr. 25 min.

   d. 5 hr. 25 min.

114. 2 hours 15 min. + 4 hours 10 min. =

   a. 7 hr. 5 min.

   b. 6 hr. 25 min.

   c. 6 hr. 5 min.

   d. 5 hr. 25 min.

115. Convert 35° Celsius into degrees Fahrenheit. Use $F = \frac{9}{5}C + 32$.

   a. 2016° F

   b. 347° F

   c. 216° F

   d. 95° F

116. What is the sum of 2 ft. 5 in., 2 yd. 1 ft. 3 in., 4 yd. 8 in., and 3 ft. 2 in.?

   a. 7 yd. 7 ft. 6 in.

   b. 6 yd. 7 ft. 6 in.

   c. 6 yd. 6 ft. 6 in.

   d. 7 yd. 7 ft. 7 in.

117. If 1' 10" is cut from a plank that is 3' 3" long, then how long is the remaining piece?

   a. 2' 7"

   b. 2' 5"

   c. 1' 7"

   d. 1' 5"

118. Reference information:

1 gallon = 4 quarts

2 pints = 1 quart

A pitcher initially contains 1 gal. 2 qt. of punch. If eight 1-pint servings are poured out, how much punch remains in the container?

   a. 4 qt.

   b. 2 pints

   c. 2 qt.

   d. 1 qt. 1 pint

119. Three feet 7 inches plus 5 feet 8 inches equals
   a. 9′ 5″
   b. 9′ 3″
   c. 8′ 5″
   d. 8′ 3″

120. Reference information:
2 cups = 1 pint
2 pints = 1 quart
4 quarts = 1 gallon

Which answer choice represents the greatest volume of liquid?
   a. 7 quarts
   b. 5 pints
   c. 3 cups
   d. 1 gallon

SET 6

121. Use the chart below to calculate the ratio of wet sand to pumice (in pounds per cubic feet).

Substance	Weight (lbs/ft³)
Pumice	40
Saltpeter	75
Sand, dry	101
Sand, wet	120

   a. 10:4
   b. 1:3
   c. 4:10
   d. 3:1

122. A hospital is collecting donations to raise funds for a new wing. According to the table below, what was Jen's donation?

Donations

Name	Amount donated
Kristi	$525
Ryan	$440
Jen	?
Toni	$615
Total	$2055

   a. 415
   b. 475
   c. 515
   d. It cannot be determined based on the information given.

123. Use the chart below to determine the mean score of the people listed.

Name	Score
Alec	75
George	81
Felicia	93
Maria	77
Ashley	84

   a. 82
   b. 102
   c. 76
   d. 89

The chart below shows revenues in millions of dollars for the three regional divisions of Stewart Financial. Use this chart to answer questions 124–125.

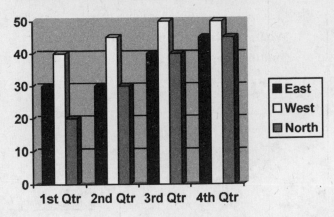

124. How many millions of dollars did the West division bring in throughout the first three quarters shown?

a. 120
b. 135
c. 185
d. 200

125. How much more did the East make in the third quarter than the North made in the first quarter?

a. 20 million dollars
b. 15 million dollars
c. 10 million dollars
d. 5 million dollars

126. Use the graph below to best approximate the amount of bacteria (in grams) present on Day 4.

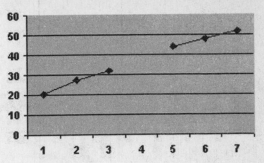

a. 48 grams
b. 38 grams
c. 28 grams
d. 18 grams

127. The graph below shows the yearly energy consumption used by Kiddie Castle Pre-school over the course of three years for three different sources of fuel. The cost for gas during the year 1997 was how much greater than the cost for oil in 1998?

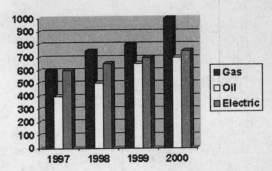

a. $200
b. $150
c. $100
d. None of the above. The cost for oil was greater.

128. Use the chart below to determine which answer choice(s) represents a true statement.

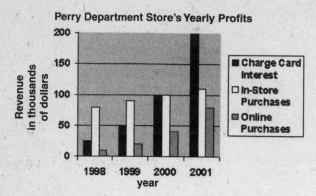

Perry Department Store's Yearly Profits

a. The dollar amount made on in-store purchases has doubled every year since 1998.

b. The dollar amount made from online purchases has doubled every year since 1998.

c. The dollar amount made from charge card interest has doubled every year since 1998.

d. Choices b and c are true.

129. The pie chart below shows the number of employees working in each of the various departments of Montgomery Tech Inc.

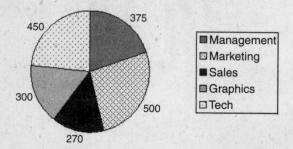

Which two departments represent 645 employees?

a. management + graphics

b. graphics + marketing

c. management + sales

d. marketing + sales

130. The student enrollment at Layfette Technical Institute is given below in the form of a three-dimensional pie chart in which students are grouped according to their course of study. What is the ratio of programming students to multimedia students?

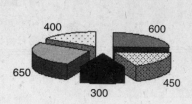
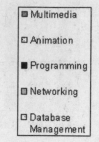

a. 2:1

b. 1:2

c. 4:6

d. 3:4

S·E·C·T·I·O·N

FRACTIONS

2

Fractions permeate any type of math question you can think of. They're in proportion questions, geometry questions, chart questions, mean questions, ratio questions, and so on. This section contains sets that start off with elementary fraction questions, and works up to tougher fraction problems. Five sets are presented to build your competence when dealing with fractions—no matter where they turn up.

SET 7

131. What fraction of the figure below is shaded?

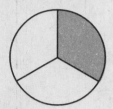

a. $\frac{1}{2}$

b. $\frac{1}{3}$

c. $\frac{2}{3}$

d. $\frac{1}{4}$

132. What fraction of the figure below is shaded?

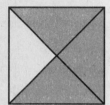

a. $\frac{1}{2}$

b. $\frac{2}{3}$

c. $\frac{2}{4}$

d. $\frac{3}{4}$

133. What fraction of the figure below is shaded?

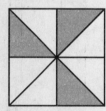

a. $\frac{1}{2}$

b. $\frac{1}{4}$

c. $\frac{2}{3}$

d. $\frac{3}{8}$

134. What fraction of the figure below is shaded?

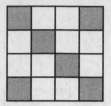

a. $\frac{5}{16}$

b. $\frac{1}{2}$

c. $\frac{3}{8}$

d. $\frac{3}{4}$

135. What fraction of the figure below is shaded?

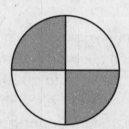

a. $\frac{1}{2}$

b. $\frac{1}{3}$

c. $\frac{1}{4}$

d. $\frac{3}{4}$

136. Change $\frac{132}{12}$ to a whole number.

a. 8

b. 11

c. 18

d. 32

137. The mixed number $3\frac{2}{3}$ is equivalent to which improper fraction below?

a. $\frac{6}{3}$

b. $\frac{9}{3}$

c. $\frac{11}{3}$

d. $\frac{13}{3}$

138. Express $\frac{12}{4}$ as a whole number.
a. 8
b. 4
c. 3
d. 2

139. Convert $1\frac{5}{7}$ to an improper fraction.
a. $\frac{12}{7}$
b. $\frac{6}{7}$
c. $\frac{2}{14}$
d. $\frac{5}{14}$

140. The reciprocal of $2\frac{1}{3}$ is
a. $\frac{7}{3}$
b. 1
c. $-2\frac{1}{3}$
d. $\frac{3}{7}$

141. Which of the following choices is an improper fraction?
a. $\frac{18}{36}$
b. $\frac{93}{57}$
c. $\frac{21}{80}$
d. $\frac{121}{300}$

142. Which of the following has the greatest value?
a. $\frac{5}{8}$
b. $\frac{2}{3}$
c. $\frac{8}{11}$
d. $\frac{4}{10}$

143. Which of the following is between $\frac{1}{4}$ and $\frac{2}{3}$?
a. $\frac{5}{8}$
b. $\frac{5}{6}$
c. $\frac{8}{11}$
d. $\frac{7}{10}$

144. Express this improper fraction as a mixed number: $\frac{17}{3}$
a. $5\frac{1}{3}$
b. $5\frac{2}{3}$
c. $2\frac{1}{5}$
d. $2\frac{3}{5}$

145. $\frac{15}{2}$ is equivalent to the mixed number
a. $3\frac{1}{5}$
b. $5\frac{1}{2}$
c. $7\frac{1}{2}$
d. $8\frac{1}{2}$

SET 8

146. $\frac{1}{9} + \frac{5}{9} =$
a. $\frac{4}{9}$
b. $\frac{7}{9}$
c. $\frac{1}{3}$
d. $\frac{2}{3}$

147. $\frac{5}{8} - \frac{3}{8} =$
a. $-\frac{2}{8}$
b. $\frac{2}{3}$
c. $\frac{1}{4}$
d. $\frac{1}{8}$

148. $\frac{5}{9} - \frac{1}{4} =$
a. $\frac{11}{36}$
b. $\frac{4}{5}$
c. $\frac{3}{4}$
d. $\frac{5}{18}$

149. $9\frac{5}{6} - 7\frac{1}{8} =$
a. $\frac{29}{24}$
b. $2\frac{17}{24}$
c. $2\frac{5}{8}$
d. $\frac{13}{12}$

150. $-\frac{3}{7} - \frac{4}{7} =$

  a. 1
  b. -1
  c. $-\frac{1}{7}$
  d. $\frac{1}{7}$

151. $\left(-\frac{2}{5}\right) - \frac{3}{7} =$

  a. $-\frac{6}{35}$
  b. $\frac{29}{35}$
  c. $\frac{6}{35}$
  d. $-\frac{29}{35}$

152. $1\frac{2}{7} + \frac{1}{9} =$

  a. $1\frac{3}{16}$
  b. $1\frac{3}{9}$
  c. $1\frac{25}{63}$
  d. $1\frac{24}{35}$

153. $2\frac{5}{8} + 3\frac{1}{4} - 5\frac{5}{6} =$

  a. $-\frac{181}{24}$
  b. $10\frac{10}{18}$
  c. $\frac{1}{24}$
  d. $2\frac{3}{18}$

154. $\frac{5}{8} \times \frac{4}{7} =$

  a. $\frac{5}{14}$
  b. $\frac{20}{8}$
  c. $\frac{25}{32}$
  d. $\frac{9}{16}$

155. $2\frac{2}{3} \times 8\frac{1}{5} =$

  a. $16\frac{2}{15}$
  b. $18\frac{7}{15}$
  c. $19\frac{13}{15}$
  d. $21\frac{13}{15}$

156. $2\frac{3}{5} \times 1\frac{2}{3} =$

  a. $2\frac{6}{15}$
  b. $4\frac{1}{3}$
  c. $3\frac{7}{15}$
  d. $4\frac{2}{3}$

157. $-2\frac{5}{7} \times 4\frac{1}{5} =$

  a. $11\frac{2}{5}$
  b. $8\frac{1}{7}$
  c. $-11\frac{2}{5}$
  d. $-8\frac{1}{7}$

158. Using the formula *Area = length × width*, what is the area of the rectangle below?

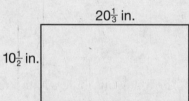

$20\frac{1}{3}$ in.

$10\frac{1}{2}$ in.

  a. $30\frac{2}{5}$ in^2
  b. $180\frac{1}{2}$ in^2
  c. $200\frac{1}{6}$ in^2
  d. $213\frac{1}{2}$ in^2

159. What is the reciprocal of $\frac{21}{42}$?

  a. $\frac{1}{2}$
  b. $-\frac{21}{42}$
  c. $-\frac{1}{2}$
  d. $\frac{42}{21}$

160. $5 \div \frac{2}{7} =$

  a. $17\frac{1}{2}$
  b. $10\frac{2}{7}$
  c. $\frac{10}{7}$
  d. $\frac{2}{35}$

161. $\frac{18}{5} \div \frac{9}{20}$
    a. $\frac{63}{100}$
    b. $\frac{300}{45}$
    c. 8
    d. 10

162. $1\frac{2}{7} \div \frac{9}{11}$
    a. $9\frac{4}{7}$
    b. $1\frac{4}{7}$
    c. $9\frac{18}{77}$
    d. $1\frac{77}{18}$

163. Divide $1\frac{3}{8}$ by $1\frac{1}{4}$.
    a. $1\frac{1}{40}$
    b. $1\frac{1}{3}$
    c. $1\frac{1}{10}$
    d. $1\frac{1}{4}$

164. $6 \div \frac{12}{13} =$
    a. $2\frac{1}{13}$
    b. $4\frac{1}{12}$
    c. $4\frac{3}{4}$
    d. $6\frac{1}{2}$

165. $3\frac{1}{3} \div \frac{5}{9} =$
    a. $\frac{6}{15}$
    b. 6
    c. $15\frac{1}{3}$
    d. 15

SET 9

Use the chart below to answer Questions 166–168.

Laurie's Jogging Log

Day	Miles jogged
Sunday	4
Monday	3
Tuesday	$3\frac{1}{3}$
Wednesday	5
Thursday	$2\frac{1}{3}$
Friday	$2\frac{2}{3}$
Saturday	3

166. Which answer choice correctly expresses the difference between the amount of miles Laurie jogged on Tuesday and the amount of miles that she jogged on Thursday?
    a. $3\frac{1}{3} + 2\frac{1}{3}$
    b. $3 - 2\frac{1}{3}$
    c. $3\frac{1}{3} - 2\frac{2}{3}$
    d. $3\frac{1}{3} - 2\frac{1}{3}$

167. When the miles jogged on Thursday and Friday are combined, the resulting value is
    a. $4\frac{2}{3}$ mi.
    b. 5 mi.
    c. $5\frac{1}{3}$ mi.
    d. $5\frac{2}{3}$ mi.

168. What was Laurie's average daily jog (in miles) for the week shown in the chart above?
    a. $2\frac{2}{3}$
    b. 3
    c. $3\frac{1}{3}$
    d. $3\frac{2}{3}$

169. Which choice is an improper fraction?

   a. $\frac{7}{10}$

   b. $\frac{24}{25}$

   c. $\frac{54}{12}$

   d. $\frac{38}{40}$

170. Dividing by $\frac{3}{5}$ is the same as

   a. multiplying by 3 and dividing by 5.

   b. dividing by 5 and multiplying by 3.

   c. dividing by $\frac{5}{3}$.

   d. multiplying by $\frac{5}{3}$.

171. Sebastian is going to pay $\frac{2}{3}$ of the price of his new house in cash. His friend Rachel will loan him $\frac{1}{4}$ of the $360,000 total cost of the house. How much more money does Sebastian need in order to pay for the house in full?

   a. $30,000

   b. $45,000

   c. $60,000

   d. $90,000

172. The most basic building block in the universe, the *quark*, had its name taken from a James Joyce novel. Quarks can have the following charges: $+\frac{1}{3} -\frac{1}{3} +\frac{2}{3} -\frac{2}{3}$
If three quarks are together with charges $+\frac{2}{3}, -\frac{1}{3},$ and $+\frac{1}{3}$, what is the sum of these charges?

   a. $-\frac{4}{3}$

   b. $\frac{4}{3}$

   c. $-\frac{2}{3}$

   d. $\frac{2}{3}$

173. Greg completes $\frac{3}{4}$ of his data entry assignment in 45 minutes. How long, in *hours*, does it take him to complete the whole assignment?

   a. 1 hr.

   b. 1 hr. 20 min.

   c. $1\frac{1}{2}$ hr.

   d. $1\frac{3}{4}$ hr.

174. If a delivery of bolts is $3\frac{1}{2}$ gross, how many bolts are there? *Note*: 1 gross = 144 units.

   a. 178

   b. 216

   c. 432

   d. 504

175. Jane is $\frac{1}{3}$ of Zoey's age and she is half as old as Jaclyn. If Jaclyn is 16, how old is Zoey?

   a. 8

   b. 12

   c. 16

   d. 24

SET 10

Use the chart below to answer Questions 176–177.

Average Yearly Costs of Common Home Appliances

Appliance	Energy (kwh)	Cost per year @ 12¢ per kwh
Washer	150	$18
Dryer	1000	$120
Air Conditioner	1500	$180
Television (in use 8 hrs a day)	1000	$120

Note: kwh = kilowatt hour

176. How much money would Allison have to spend on the energy used for her television each year if she leaves it on for 5 hours a day?

   a. $112

   b. $75

   c. $60

   d. $40

177. Suppose that in New York the cost per kwh is raised by $\frac{1}{4}$, and that in Florida, the cost per kwh is raised by $\frac{1}{8}$. In comparing the *annual* cost for the energy used to run a dryer, how much more would it cost the average New Yorker than the average Florida resident?

a. $10
b. $15
c. $20
d. It cannot be determined by the information given.

178. The design for a sculpture is represented in the diagram below. If the diagram is drawn to scale, and the base will be $8\frac{1}{2}$ inches tall when the sculpture is built, how tall will the actual tower be?

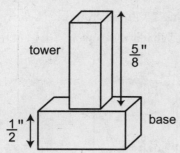

a. $16\frac{1}{4}$ in.
b. $12\frac{5}{8}$ in.
c. $10\frac{5}{8}$ in.
d. $8\frac{1}{4}$ in.

179. Which answer choice represents the number missing from the pattern below?

$\frac{1}{8}$ $\frac{1}{16}$ $\frac{1}{32}$ ____ $\frac{1}{128}$

a. 64
b. 100
c. $\frac{1}{64}$
d. $\frac{1}{100}$

180. Starting with a full 200-gallon gas tank, Vincent will use $7\frac{5}{8}$ gal/day. How many days will it take until his tank contains 17 gallons?

a. $26\frac{14}{61}$ days
b. $25\frac{1}{8}$ days
c. 24 days
d. It cannot be determined by the information given.

181. Cathy earns $60,000 a year. Darlene's yearly earnings are $\frac{1}{3}$ more than Cathy's. If Denise's stock portfolio is worth $\frac{1}{5}$ of what Darlene earns each year, how much is her stock portfolio worth?

a. $900,000
b. $24,000
c. $16,000
d. $4,000

182. Sky, Gina, and Margaret combined their savings to start a business. At the end of the year, Sky will get $\frac{1}{7}$ of the profits, Gina will get $\frac{2}{7}$ of the profits, Margaret will get $\frac{3}{7}$ of the profits, and $\frac{1}{7}$ of the profits will get donated to charity. Last year, Margaret received $12,240 profit at the end of the year. What was the *total* profit for last year?

a. $85,680
b. $48,960
c. $36,720
d. $28,560

183. There were 504 candies in a jar. Between 8 o'clock and 9 o'clock, $\frac{1}{8}$ of the candies were given out. Between 9 o'clock and 10 o'clock, $\frac{2}{9}$ of the remaining candies were handed out. If, in the following hour, $\frac{1}{7}$ of the remaining candies are distributed, how many candies will be left?

    a. 336

    b. 294

    c. 188

    d. 96

184. This week, Brian will work $\frac{2}{5}$ of his usual 30-hour workweek. If he makes $14 per hour, how much will he earn this week (before taxes)?

    a. $420

    b. $252

    c. $168

    d. $116

185. Rayeel jogs at a rate of $5\frac{1}{3}$ miles per hour. If he just jogged 16 miles, how many hours has he jogged so far?

    a. 3 hours

    b. $3\frac{1}{3}$ hours

    c. $3\frac{2}{3}$ hours

    d. 4 hours

186. If Cassidy spends $\frac{1}{4}$ of her vacation funds on Monday and $\frac{1}{3}$ of the remainder on Tuesday, what fraction of her original fund remains?

    a. $\frac{1}{4}$

    b. $\frac{1}{2}$

    c. $\frac{3}{4}$

    d. $\frac{2}{3}$

187. Use the chart below to answer the following question: The decibel value for normal speech is what fraction of the decibel value for a noise that would incur hearing loss?

Sound	Decibels (dB)
Normal Speech	50
Lawn Mower	100
Rocket Launch	140
Loss of Hearing	150

    a. $\frac{2}{1}$

    b. $\frac{3}{1}$

    c. $\frac{1}{3}$

    d. $\frac{1}{2}$

SET 11

188. After adding 20 L, the container below will be totally full. What is the capacity (in L) of the container?

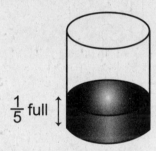

$\frac{1}{5}$ full

    a. 100 L

    b. 25 L

    c. 20 L

    d. It cannot be determined based on the information given.

189. A model statue is $4\frac{1}{2}''$ tall. If it was built to scale, such that $\frac{1}{2}$ inch represents 1 foot, which proportion below can be used to solve for the height (in feet) of the actual statue?

a. $\dfrac{\frac{1}{1}}{\frac{1}{2}} = \dfrac{4\frac{1}{2}}{height}$

b. $\dfrac{\frac{1}{2}}{1} = \dfrac{height}{4\frac{1}{2}}$

c. $\dfrac{\frac{1}{2}}{1} = \dfrac{12}{height}$

d. $\dfrac{\frac{1}{2}}{1} = \dfrac{4\frac{1}{2}}{height}$

190. Camille was hired to hang 64 flyers around the city. If she completed $\frac{3}{4}$ of her task, how many flyers still need to be hung?

a. 48

b. 32

c. 24

d. 16

191. A recipe calls for $\frac{1}{2}$ tsp. of coriander and serves 4 people. If Heather needs to cook for 24 people, how much coriander does she need?

a. 3 tsp.

b. $3\frac{1}{2}$ tsp.

c. 4 tsp.

d. 6 tsp.

192. Suppose that in the question above, Heather needs to prepare enough food for 26 people. How much coriander should she add?

a. $3\frac{1}{4}$ tsp

b. $3\frac{1}{2}$ tsp

c. $4\frac{3}{4}$ tsp

d. $6\frac{1}{4}$ tsp

193. A flight that takes 12 hours is currently $3\frac{1}{8}$ hours into the trip. In how many hours will the plane land?

a. $9\frac{1}{8}$

b. $8\frac{7}{8}$

c. $8\frac{1}{8}$

d. $7\frac{7}{8}$

194. Faleena was assigned a 110-question take home test over the weekend. On Friday night, she completed $\frac{1}{5}$ of the test. On Saturday, she finished $\frac{1}{4}$ of the remainder. On Sunday morning, she completed $\frac{1}{3}$ of the remaining questions. How many questions does she have left?

a. 23

b. 32

c. 44

d. 51

195. Evelyn lent a quarter of her paycheck to A.J. and spent a third of it on a dinner with Jim. How much of her paycheck does she have left to spend?

a. half of her paycheck

b. three quarters of her paycheck

c. two ninths of her paycheck

d. five twelfths of her paycheck

196. Energy costs at Redfield Lumber totaled $680 for March. One quarter of this cost was for oil heating. Which expression represents the amount spent on oil heating in March?

a. $680 \div \frac{1}{4}$

b. 680×4

c. $\dfrac{680}{\frac{1}{4}}$

d. $\dfrac{680}{4}$

197. Danny addressed 14 out of 42 envelopes. What fraction of the envelopes still need to be addressed?

a. $\frac{23}{42}$

b. $\frac{13}{21}$

c. $\frac{2}{3}$

d. $\frac{4}{7}$

198. If Samantha ate $\frac{1}{3}$ of a pizza and Melissa ate $\frac{1}{4}$ of the remainder, how much of the original pie is left?

a. $\frac{1}{12}$

b. $\frac{1}{2}$

c. $\frac{1}{4}$

d. $\frac{5}{12}$

199. A three-quart container is completely filled with a 50-50 mixture of juice and water. If one third of the mixture is poured out and one quart of juice is added, how much juice is in the resulting mixture?

a. 2 qt.

b. $2\frac{1}{2}$ qt.

c. $2\frac{1}{3}$ qt.

d. It cannot be determined based on the information given.

200. At a computer show, Wahl Tech was handing out free trial disks. By 1 o'clock, $\frac{2}{5}$ were handed out. By 3 o'clock, $\frac{1}{3}$ of the remaining disks were handed out. What fraction of the original disks remains at this point?

a. $\frac{7}{15}$

b. $\frac{1}{3}$

c. $\frac{6}{15}$

d. $\frac{1}{15}$

Use the diagram below to answer questions 201–202.

Daily U.S. Water Usage per Person

| ■ Industrial 3800 L |
| □ Agriculture 2150 L |
| ▨ Nonindustrial 550 L |

201. What fractional part of water usage per person does "nonindustrial" represent?

a. $\frac{38}{65}$

b. $\frac{43}{130}$

c. $\frac{11}{130}$

d. $\frac{55}{330}$

202. Suppose the daily average industrial usage was decreased by $\frac{4}{5}$. How many liters per person, on average, would the new industrial value be?

a. 3040 L

b. 2300 L

c. 1500 L

d. 760 L

S·E·C·T·I·O·N 3
DECIMALS

These sets deal with decimals and scientific notation. You will see questions that involve operations with decimals, comparisons, conversion to fractions, and operations involving scientific notation and exponents. Decimals turn up in proportion questions, series questions, unit conversion questions, and just about any type of math question you can think of. Work through these six sets to get a sampling of question types as you sharpen your skills in dealing with decimals.

SET 12

203. What is the value of 6.567 − 5.291?
a. 12.76
b. 11.858
c. 1.276
d. 1.1858

204. What is the value of 3.411 + 7.83562?
a. 7.86973
b. 11.24662
c. 78.6973
d. 112.4662

205. 563.9817 − 61.935 =
a. 557.7882
b. 502.0467
c. 55.77882
d. 50.20467

206. Adam collected the following amounts of change from under all of his living room furniture: .24, .75, .89, and 1.27. What was the total amount of change he found?
a. 315
b. 31.5
c. 3.15
d. .315

207. Which of the following choices has a six in the hundredths place?
a. .69573
b. .93657
c. .96357
d. .93576

208. 43.071 + 22.823 =
a. 65.894
b. 658.94
c. 6.5894
d. .65894

209. 6.7 − 2.135 =
a. 4.656
b. .4656
c. .4565
d. 4.565

210. −4.257 + .23 =
a. −4.487
b. −4.027
c. 4.487
d. 4.027

211. 18.731 − 2.04 =
a. 18.527
b. 1.8527
c. 16.691
d. 1.6691

212. Add 25.25, 301.03, 4.001, 152, and 3.414.
a. 485.695
b. 401.95
c. 48.5695
d. 40.195

213. .532 × .89 =
a. 473.48
b. 47.348
c. 4.7348
d. .47348

214. 3.02 × 4.1 =
a. 1.2382
b. 12.382
c. 123.82
d. 1238.2

215. 7.12 × 3 =
a. 21.63
b. 216.3
c. 21.36
d. 213.6

216. .21 × .11 =
  a. 231
  b. 23.1
  c. .231
  d. .0231

217. 0.13 × 0.62 =
  a. 0.0806
  b. 0.806
  c. 8.06
  d. 80.6

218. What is the value at point A?

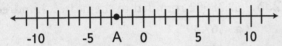

  a. 2.5
  b. −2.5
  c. −1.5
  d. −3.5

SET 13

219. Which of the following choices represents the largest value?
  a. $\frac{12}{25}$
  b. $\frac{11}{30}$
  c. $\frac{9}{15}$
  d. $\frac{4}{11}$

220. 117.3285 when rounded to the nearest hundredth is
  a. 100
  b. 117.3
  c. 117.33
  d. 117.329

221. Which number sentence is true?
  a. .52 < .0052
  b. .52 < .052
  c. .00052 > .052
  d. .052 > .0052

222. Which number sentence below is correct?
  a. .0071 > .71
  b. .071 < .00071
  c. .071 > .0071
  d. .71 < .071

223. Expressed in words, the decimal 0.005 is the same as
  a. five thousands.
  b. five hundredths.
  c. five ten thousandths.
  d. five thousandths.

224. What is .821 when rounded to the nearest tenth?
  a. .8
  b. 1
  c. .82
  d. .9

225. Which of the following numbers is between −.01 and 1.01?
  a. −.015
  b. −.005
  c. 1.5
  d. 1.15

226. Which value is equivalent to $\frac{5}{8} - \frac{2}{5}$?
  a. −.25
  b. .225
  c. .25
  d. .275

227. What is eight and seven thousandths written as a decimal?
- a. 8.7
- b. 8.07
- c. 8.007
- d. 8.0007

228. Which of the following has a seven in the ten-thousandths place?
- a. 5.7
- b. 5.27
- c. 5.127
- d. 5.0127

229. .4759 rounded to the nearest hundredth is
- a. .476
- b. .47
- c. .48
- d. .4

230. Which of the following number sentences is true?
- a. .147 > 1.02
- b. .12 > 1.4
- c. 1.2 > .43
- d. .103 > .325

231. What is the decimal form of the fraction $\frac{6}{7}$ when rounded to the nearest hundredth?
- a. .8571428
- b. .857
- c. .86
- d. .8

232. Which digit is in the thousandths place of the number 4173.2501?
- a. 0
- b. 1
- c. 2
- d. 5

233. Which of the decimals below has the *least* value?
- a. .089
- b. .0089
- c. .89
- d. .809

234. $\frac{31}{50}$ is equivalent to which of the following decimals?
- a. .315
- b. .62
- c. .155
- d. .3

235. 67.38902 rounded to the nearest hundredth is
- a. 67.3
- b. 67.38
- c. 67.39
- d. 67.389

236. Which of the following has the greatest value?
- a. 3.083
- b. 3.308
- c. 3.830
- d. 3.038

SET 14

237. Multiply 17.12 by 34.15
- a. 584.648
- b. 58.4648
- c. 5846.48
- d. 58464.8

238. .0000321 is equivalent to
- a. 3.21×10^{-6}
- b. 3.21×10^{-5}
- c. 3.21×10^{6}
- d. 3.21×10^{5}

239. $(3.09 \times 10^{12}) \div 3 =$
a. 1.03×10^4
b. 3.09×10^4
c. 1.03×10^{12}
d. 1.03×3.33^{12}

240. 6.22×10^4 can be rewritten as
a. 62200
b. 622000
c. 6220
d. .000622

241. $168 \div .056 =$
a. 9.408
b. 94.08
c. 300
d. 3000

242. $.209 \div .038 =$
a. .55
b. .65
c. 5.5
d. 6.5

243. $70 \div 3.5 =$
a. 20
b. 15
c. 2
d. 1.5

244. $1.55 \div .31 =$
a. 20
b. 15
c. 5
d. .5

245. $\frac{2.3 \times 10^4}{1.15 \times 10^8} =$
a. 2×10^4
b. 2×10^{-4}
c. 2×10^{-8}
d. 2×10^8

246. $(3.2 \times 10^{-3})(2.4 \times 10^5) =$
a. 7.68×10^2
b. 7.68×10^{-2}
c. $.768 \times 10^2$
d. $.768 \times 10^{-2}$

247. 5.4321 multiplied by 10^{-5} is equal to
a. 543210
b. 54321
c. 0.00054321
d. .000054321

248. 1.43×10^3 can be rewritten as
a. .00143
b. .143
c. 14.3
d. 1430

249. $\frac{6.6 \times 10^{-2}}{3.3 \times 10^5} =$
a. 2×10^7
b. 2×10^{-7}
c. 2×10^{-3}
d. 2×10^3

SET 15

250. If six students pay equal amounts for materials needed for a project, how much money would each student pay if the total cost of materials was $27.90?
a. $4.50
b. $4.65
c. $6.75
d. $6.80

251. In New York, there is no sales tax on clothes. Jessica Lyn spent $14.50 on a knit shirt, $4.25 on a scarf, $22.80 on a jacket, and $32.60 on a pair of jeans. How much did she spend altogether?
   a. $7415
   b. $741.5
   c. $74.15
   d. $7.415

252. If six bags of seed are spread evenly over an area of 315.6 square feet, what is the area (in square feet) that one bag of seed covers?
   a. 48.7
   b. 52.6
   c. 60.15
   d. 70.2

253. $480.85 is to be divided equally among four people. To the nearest cent, how many dollars will each person get?
   a. $120.2125
   b. $120.212
   c. $120.21
   d. $120.2

254. Everyday before going to work, Tranessa stops at a gourmet coffee shop and spends $1.52 on coffee, $1.75 on a muffin, and leaves a $1 tip. If Tranessa works five days a week, how much money does Tranessa spend at this gourmet coffee shop in four weeks?
   a. $128.10
   b. $92.52
   c. $88.20
   d. $85.40

255. Which answer choice best expresses the number of centimeters that there are in a yard if there are 2.54 cm in an inch?

Reference information:
1 foot = 12 inches
3 feet = 1 yard

   a. 2.54×36
   b. $2.54 \div 12 \times 3$
   c. $12 \times 3 \div 2.54$
   d. $3 \div 2.54$

256. At a restaurant, the help earns $50.34, $63.25, and $44.30 in tips. If the total amount of money must be divided evenly among three workers, each worker will get how much money?
   a. $56.32
   b. $52.63
   c. $48.50
   d. $46.34

257. If the mass calculated by a student is considered acceptable if it is ±.02 g. within the actual weight, then which of the following students calculated an acceptable value for a mass with an actual value of 4.52 g.?

Student	Mass Calculated
Brian	4.55
Anthony	4.51
Danielle	4.32
Vincent	4.02

   a. Brian
   b. Anthony
   c. Danielle
   d. Vincent

258. If colored paper clips cost $1.25 per 100 count, which proportion can be used to calculate the amount of money (in *dollars*) that 556 paper clips would represent?

   a. $\frac{125}{100} = \frac{x}{556}$

   b. $\frac{100}{125} = \frac{x}{556}$

   c. $\frac{1.25}{100} = \frac{x}{556}$

   d. $\frac{100}{1.25} = \frac{x}{556}$

259. If tofu costs $1.50 a pound, how much will $6\frac{1}{2}$ pounds of tofu cost?

   a. $9.75

   b. $11.25

   c. $12.50

   d. $13.25

260. One book weighs 1.25 lbs. If an entire crate of books weighs 192 lbs., and the crate itself weighs 14.5 lbs., how many books are in the crate?

   a. 164

   b. 153.6 books

   c. 142 books

   d. It cannot be determined by the information given.

SET 16

261. Sean calculated that a mass weighed 45.2 grams. Athena weighed the same mass, but came up with a value of 43.7. What is the difference between these two values?

   a. 2.75 g.

   b. 2.5 g.

   c. 1.75 g.

   d. 1.5 g.

262. Plaster costs $2.45 a pound, and Stephanie needs eight pounds of plaster. If she has $13.45 in her wallet, how much more money does she need?

   a. $6.15

   b. $12.00

   c. $14.45

   d. $19.60

263. What number is missing from the series below?
8.60 8.45 ___ 8.15 8

   a. 8.40

   b. 8.35

   c. 8.30

   d. 8.25

264. Fasteners come in packs of 100. While bored at the office one day, Henry calculates that he has 3.52 boxes of fasteners. How many fasteners does Henry have?

   a. 360

   b. 352

   c. 340

   d. 336

265. A large jar of olives costs $5.49 and provides enough olives to garnish 30 salads. What is the approximate cost of the olives used on 11 salads?

   a. $3.50

   b. $3.00

   c. $2.50

   d. $2.00

266. Arrange the following numbers in order from least to greatest:
5.025, 5.12, 5.251, 5.03, 5.003

   a. 5.251, 5.12, 5.03, 5.025, 5.003

   b. 5.003, 5.025, 5.12, 5.03, 5.251

   c. 5.003, 5.025, 5.03, 5.12, 5.251

   d. 5.003, 5.251, 5.12, 5.03, 5.025

267. Corrine stacks four boxes on a pull cart. The weights of the boxes are: 8.25 lbs., 10.4 lbs., 7.5 lbs., and 6.25 lbs. How much weight is on the pull cart?

a. 32.4 lbs.

b. 33.2 lbs.

c. 34.4 lbs.

d. 36.2 lbs.

268. Selena spends $15.99, $13.99, $12.99, and $25.44 on software. She also buys a phone for $45.59. If the total tax for her purchase is $9.44, and she pays with three fifty-dollar bills, what is her change?

a. $22.56

b. $26.56

c. $36.00

d. $85.59

269. A 25-lb. sack of rock salt costs $3.00. How much does rock salt cost per pound?

a. .75

b. .63

c. .31

d. .12

270. According to the Department of Agriculture, it takes 23 gallons of water to produce one pound of tomatoes, and 5214 gallons of water to produce one pound of beef. How much more water is used to produce 1.5 pounds of beef than to produce 150 pounds of tomatoes?

a. 5,200 gallons

b. 4,371 gallons

c. 3,261 gallons

d. 2,854 gallons

271. An 8-lb. crate contains two 25-lb. monitors and three 7.5-lb.. towers. What is the total weight of the entire load?

a. 40.5 lbs.

b. 60.5 lbs.

c. 80.5 lbs.

d. 100.5 lbs.

272. Matthew painted 72 rooms over the course of 5 days. What was the average number of rooms he painted per day?

a. 14.4 rooms

b. 15 rooms

c. 16.1 rooms

d. 16.3 rooms

273. While on a $100 budget, Ed spends $6.25, $13.75, and $48.40. How much money does Ed have left?

a. $68.40

b. $51.60

c. $37.85

d. $31.60

274. If 100 staples in a stick measure 2″ long, how thick is 1 staple?

a. .2 in.

b. .02 in.

c. .4 in.

d. .04 in.

275. Gel pens cost $3.50 per box. Felt-tip pens cost $2.75 per box. If Jade purchases three boxes of gel pens and two boxes of felt tip pens, how much will she spend in all?

a. $16

b. $15.25

c. $10.50

d. $5.50

SET 17

276. Use the chart below to determine what the height of the water will be at 10 A.M., given the same rate of accumulation.

Time	Water Height
5 A.M.	23.02 cm
6 A.M.	23.23 cm
7 A.M.	23.44 cm

a. 23.65 cm
b. 24.02 cm
c. 24.07 cm
d. 26.21 cm

277. How much will Jill save by purchasing the All-In-One model instead of purchasing a printer, fax, scanner, and copy machine separately? Refer to the price list below.

Price List	
Printer	$252.49
Fax	$149.99
Scanner	$152.49
Copier	$499.99
All-In-One (printer/ fax/scanner/copier)	$799.99

a. $254.97
b. $302.57
c. $404.96
d. $1054.96

278. Reanna went to the bookstore and bought four books at an average price of $18.95. If three of the books sold for $25.25, $14.95, and $19.95, what is the cost of the fourth book?

a. $20.05
b. $18.95
c. $15.65
d. $14.25

279. Four envelopes had an equal amount of money enclosed. Clarissa then gave away one of the envelopes, and the total amount in the remaining three envelopes is $71.25. Find the sum of the money enclosed in the initial four envelopes.

a. $110.75
b. $102
c. $99.25
d. $95

280. A slab of stone weighs 48.3 pounds, and another is $\frac{1}{3}$ as heavy. What is the combined weight of the 2 slabs of stone?

a. 72.45 lbs.
b. 64.4 lbs.
c. 58 lbs.
d. 52.3 lbs.

281. 250 pieces of foil are in a stack that is half an inch tall. How thick is each piece?

a. .25 in
b. .125 in
c. .02 in
d. .002 in

282. Felicia drove at a constant rate of 50 mph during a span of 1 hour and 30 minutes. If her car gets 25 miles to the gallon, and gas costs $1.65 per gallon, how many dollars worth of gas did she consume during her drive?

a. $82.50
b. $41.25
c. $20
d. $4.95

283. The metal disk below weighs 30.48 grams. Allison slices the disk through its center into 6 equal wedges (shown below). How much will one of these wedges weigh?

   a. 5.08 g.
   b. 12.3 g.
   c. 18.29 g.
   d. 20.1 g.

284. If ice weighs .033 pounds per cubic inch, how much does it weigh per cubic foot?
   a. 4.752 lbs./ft.^{3}
   b. 20.53 lbs./ft.^{3}
   c. 57.024 lbs./ft.^{3}
   d. 73 lbs./ft.^{3}

285. Pyrite, also called fool's gold, weighs between .148 and .181 lbs. per in^3. Pure gold weighs .698 lbs. per in^3. If Block A weighs 27.92 lbs., and Block B weighs 2.4 lbs., then what conclusions can be drawn?

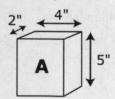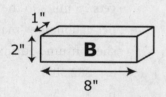

   a. Block A and Block B are both pure gold.
   b. Block A and Block B are both pyrite.
   c. Block A is pure gold and Block B is pyrite.
   d. Block A is pyrite and Block B is pure gold.

286. While on vacation, Carla would like to visit the places labeled Site A and Site B on the map below. How many miles is Site A from Site B?

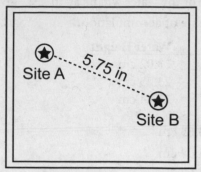

Scale .25 in = 1 mi

   a. 2.3 miles
   b. 2.5 miles
   c. 23 miles
   d. 25 miles

S·E·C·T·I·O·N

PERCENTS

4

Percents are just *hundredths*. We've seen *hundredths* when we addressed fractions and decimals. In this section, we will review how to express given percentages as both fractions and decimals. We will also compute unknown percents, as well as calculate percent increases and percent decreases, and interest. Toward the end of this section, we will tackle word problems that are part percent problems, and part algebra problems. These "hybrid" questions belong in this section because getting them correct hinges on your ability to manage percents. Remember, if your "game plan" lands you in a set that is too rough, be sure to drop down to a lower set. Here are six sets involving percents.

SET 18

287. When converted to a decimal, 35% is equivalent to
- a. .035
- b. .35
- c. 3.5
- d. 35

288. 52% can be expressed as which of the following fractions?
- a. $\frac{.52}{100}$
- b. $\frac{20}{50}$
- c. $\frac{67}{75}$
- d. $\frac{13}{25}$

289. When expressed as a percent, $\frac{42}{50}$ is equivalent to
- a. 42%
- b. $\frac{42}{50}$%
- c. 84%
- d. 90%

290. Another way to write 27.5% is
- a. $\frac{.275}{100}$
- b. $\frac{23}{80}$
- c. $\frac{11}{40}$
- d. $\frac{7}{20}$

291. Which of the following is 17% of 3400?
- a. 200
- b. 340
- c. 578
- d. 620

292. When expressed as a percent, $\frac{3}{45}$ is equivalent to
- a. .066%
- b. .06%
- c. .6%
- d. $6\frac{2}{3}$%

293. Which symbol belongs in the box below?

12.5% [ ] $\frac{3}{8}$
- a. <
- b. >
- c. =
- d. ≥

294. Express 6.2% as a fraction.
- a. $\frac{62}{100}$
- b. $\frac{31}{500}$
- c. $\frac{31}{1000}$
- d. $\frac{62}{10000}$

295. $\frac{2}{5}$% is equal to
- a. 40
- b. 4
- c. .04
- d. .004

296. $\frac{3}{24}$ is equivalent to which of the following percentages?
- a. .125%
- b. 1.25%
- c. 12.5%
- d. 125%

297. 22.5% is equivalent to
- a. 2.25
- b. .225
- c. .025
- d. .0225

SET 19

298. 400% of 30 is
- a. 1.2
- b. 12
- c. 120
- d. 1,200

299. Solve for y: $25\% = \frac{y}{40}$
  a. 10
  b. 30
  c. 300
  d. 1000

300. 112 is 80% of which of the following numbers?
  a. 89.6
  b. 122.4
  c. 140
  d. 192

301. 40% of what number is equal to 108?
  a. 43.2
  b. 86.4
  c. 172
  d. 270

302. If 25% of x is 23, then $x =$
  a. 92
  b. 88
  c. 24
  d. $5\frac{3}{4}$

303. What percentage of 40 is 32?
  a. 12.8%
  b. 25%
  c. 40%
  d. 80%

304. What percent of $\frac{8}{9}$ is $\frac{1}{3}$?
  a. $\frac{1}{3}\%$
  b. 29.6%
  c. 37.5%
  d. $40\frac{1}{3}\%$

305. What percentage of 300 is 400?
  a. 200%
  b. $133\frac{1}{3}\%$
  c. 500%
  d. 1,200%

SET 20

306. To calculate 25% of a dollar amount you can
  a. multiply the amount by 25.
  b. divide the amount by 25.
  c. multiply the amount by 4.
  d. divide the amount by 4.

307. Using the chart below, which sales people (when combined), sold 85% of the total?

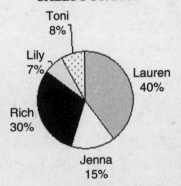

SALES FOR 2001

  a. Toni, Rich, and Jenna
  b. Rich, Lily, and Lauren
  c. Lauren, Jenna, and Rich
  d. Lily, Toni, and Rich

308. Choose the expression that can be used to solve for the following statement:
20% of $325
  a. 2×325
  b. $.02 \times 325$
  c. $2 \times .10(325)$
  d. $325 - .2(325)$

309. If the enrollment, E, at a Shaolin Kung Fu School is increased by 75%, which of the following expressions represents the new enrollment?
  a. $.75E$
  b. $E - .75E$
  c. $\frac{3}{4}E$
  d. $E + \frac{3}{4}E$

310. A 15% discount off an item that costs $V will result in a price of

a. .15V

b. 1.5V

c. .85V

d. 8.5V

311. Which proportion can be used to solve for the percent of a year that 180 days is equivalent to?

a. $\frac{180}{365} = \frac{X}{100}$

b. $\frac{180}{365} = \frac{X}{365}$

c. $\frac{180}{100} = \frac{X}{365}$

d. $\frac{365}{180} = \frac{X}{100}$

312. Taking 150% of a number is the same as

a. multiplying the number by 15.

b. increasing the number by 50%.

c. adding 1.5 times the number to itself.

d. decreasing the number by .5 times that number.

313. Given that 7% of men and 1% of women are born colorblind, use the information in the chart below to predict how many *people* in Mastic are colorblind.

Population of Mastic

Men	Women
4700	4900

a. 329

b. 378

c. 567

d. 768

314. Mary gets a 15% discount on all orders that she places at the copy store. If her orders cost $W, $X, $Y, and $Z before the discount is applied, which expression represents how much it will cost her after the discount is deducted from her total?

a. $.85(W + X + Y + Z)$

b. $.15(W + X + Y + Z)$

c. $(W + X + Y + Z) + .15(W + X + Y + Z)$

d. $(W + X + Y + Z) - 15(W + X + Y + Z)$

The pie chart below shows Charlie's monthly expenses. Use this information to answer questions 315–316 below.

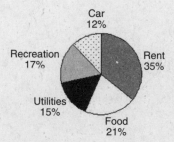

315. Which three expenses represent half of his total expenses?

a. rent and car

b. car, utilities, and recreation

c. car, food, and recreation

d. food and rent

316. If Charlie's total expenses are $1,500 per month, how much does he spend on food over the course of *two* months?

a. $270

b. $315

c. $420

d. $630

317. The chart below shows the percent composition of the human body with respect to various elements. What is the value of *x*?

Element	Percent by Weight
Carbon	18%
Hydrogen	10%
Oxygen	65%
Other Elements	*x*%
Total	**100%**

a. 5

b. 7

c. 17

d. 25

318. Use the chart below to calculate the percent increase in oil cost from 1997 to 1998.

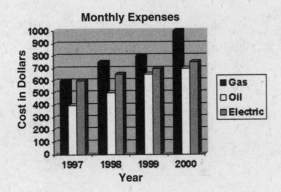

a. 25%

b. 50%

c. 75%

d. 100%

319. The pie chart below shows the percent sales for TrueTech. If sales totaled $270,000, how much money did the Overseas division bring in?

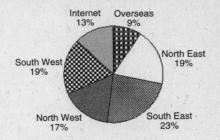

a. $243,000

b. $51,300

c. $24,300

d. $5,130

320. A small business is looking to set up a network of computers in its office. Four companies gave the original price quotes indicated in the chart below, followed by a second price quote at a later date. Based on the second price quote, which company is offering the lowest price?

	Original Quote	Second Quote
K Tech	$12,000	decrease original quote by $\frac{1}{4}$
L Tech	$13,400	75% of original quote
M Tech	$11,500	less 15% from original quote
N Tech	$15,000	$\frac{7}{8}$ of original offer

a. K Tech

b. L Tech

c. M Tech

d. N Tech

SET 21

321. Use the pie chart below to calculate the number of people working in the Management division, if the total staff is 18,950.

Division of Staff

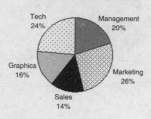

- a. 4,927
- b. 4,548
- c. 3,890
- d. 3,790

322. Use the chart below to calculate the percent increase in profits made on charge card interest from 1999 to 2001.

Yearly Profits for Perry's Department Stores

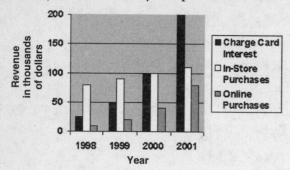

- a. 3%
- b. 50%
- c. 150%
- d. 300%

323. Malone Co. stocks averaged $12.45 per share for April. In May, the stocks averaged 14% higher. Which expression represents the average value of stocks for May?
- a. $12.45 - .14(12.45)$
- b. $1.14(12.45)$
- c. $12.45 + .14(12.45)$
- d. Both **b** and **c** are correct.

324. Which proportion represents the percent of a week that 4 days is equivalent to?
- a. $\frac{7}{4} = \frac{x}{100}$
- b. $\frac{4}{7} = \frac{x}{100}$
- c. $\frac{4}{7} = \frac{x}{30}$
- d. $\frac{7}{30} = \frac{x}{100}$

325. Two brothers decide to divide the entire cost of taking their father out to dinner evenly among the two of them. If the three meals cost a, b, and c dollars, and a 15% tip will be added in for the waiter, which equation shows how much each brother will spend?
- a. $.15(a + b + c) \div 2$
- b. $\frac{1.15(a + b + c)}{2}$
- c. $\frac{(a + b + c) + .15(a + b + c)}{2}$
- d. Both **b** and **c** are true.

326. A scanner that sells for $448 is on sale for 15% off. Which expression represents the new price of the scanner?
- a. $448 - 15$
- b. $.15(448)$
- c. $448 - .15(448)$
- d. $1.5(448)$

327. Use the formula $I = PRT$ to answer the following question. How long will $3,200 have to be invested at 8% to earn $768 in interest?

a. 1 year
b. 2 years
c. 3 years
d. 4 years

328. If Jean puts $10,000 in the bank at a 6% rate of interest, how much interest will she make in 8 months? Use the formula $I = PRT$.

a. $400
b. $350
c. $300
d. $250

329. If the volume in a water tank, V, is increased by 25%, which of the following expressions represents the new volume of water?

a. $V + \frac{1}{4}V$
b. $1.25V$
c. $V + .25V$
d. All of the above choices are correct.

330. Use the chart below to determine which answer choice contains an expression that can be used to solve for the percent increase, I, in the speed of sound through air at 100°C as compared with the speed of sound through air at 0°C.

Medium	Speed of sound (m/s)
Air 0°C	331
Air 20°C	343
Air 100°C	366

a. $\frac{12}{331} = \frac{I}{100}$
b. $\frac{35}{331} = \frac{I}{100}$
c. $\frac{35}{366} = \frac{I}{100}$
d. $\frac{12}{343} = \frac{I}{100}$

SET 22

331. Which of the following is 15% of 360?

a. 60
b. 54
c. 42
d. 36

332. 40% of what number is equal to 230?

a. 575
b. 350
c. 225
d. 92

333. 23% of 441 =

a. 2,100
b. 1,014.3
c. 210
d. 101.43

334. Which of the following is 8% of 5% of 4,000?

a. 1,600
b. 160
c. 16
d. 1.6

335. Out of 750 bags of cement, 60 are damaged. What percent of the bags are in good condition?

a. 8%
b. 80%
c. 92%
d. 94%

336. Doug makes a 12% commission on every vacuum he sells. If he sold $4,000 worth of vacuums over the course of three months, what was his commission on these sales?

a. $4,480
b. $3,520
c. $800
d. $480

337. Erika's dental bill was $540. So far, she has paid 30%. How much does she still owe?

a. $162

b. $378

c. $37.80

d. $16.20

338. Joyce withdrew 15% of her available funds. If she now has $12,070 available in her account, how much did she have initially?

a. $18,105

b. $14,200

c. $1,810.50

d. $1,420

339. First aid kits cost $6.00 each. However, if Marguerite orders 100 or more, she gets a 20% discount. How much will it cost to purchase 150 first aid kits?

a. $180

b. $360

c. $720

d. $900

340. If one out of 250,000 babies is born with two different colored eyes, what percent of the population is born with two different colored eyes?

a. 4%

b. .04%

c. .004%

d. .0004%

341. As part of market research, 2 different shirts were offered to the public for free. 330 people chose the shirt with the black logo, and 170 people chose the shirt with the blue logo. What percentage of the distributed shirts had the blue logo?

a. 34%

b. 51.5%

c. 66%

d. 70%

342. After deducting 14.5% in taxes from a yearly salary of $42,500 the net amount made is

a. $36,337.50

b. $33,637.50

c. $33,337.50

d. $33,335

SET 23

343. The pie chart below represents John's monthly expenses which total $2,000. How much does John spend on his car each month?

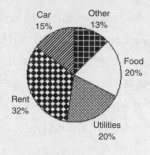

a. $220

b. $300

c. $320

d. $360

344. During the holiday season, monthly sales were calculated to be at $450,000, which was a 125% increase over prior months. How much was made during those prior months?

a. $36,000
b. $56,250
c. $112,500
d. $360,000

345. After deducting 40% in taxes, Anna took home a cash prize of $18,000. How much did she originally win?

a. $36,000
b. $30,000
c. $24,000
d. $20,000

346. Use the chart below to calculate the number of programmers at Drake Technologies, if the total number of staff members is 1,400.

DIVISION OF STAFF AT DRAKE TECHNOLOGIES

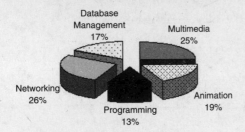

Database Management 17%
Multimedia 25%
Networking 26%
Programming 13%
Animation 19%

a. 182
b. 266
c. 350
d. 364

347. In order to get certified, a candidate must pass a 65-question exam with a minimum of 80% correct. What is the minimum number of questions Jack needs to get right in order to pass?

a. $.8 \times 65$
b. 80×65
c. $65 \div .8$
d. $.080 \times 65$

348. 800 files need to be put away. So far, Erik put away 120 files. What percent of the files did he put away?

a. $6\frac{2}{3}\%$
b. 15%
c. 18%
d. 30%

349. During the first half of a basketball game, Casey scored 15 baskets out of 20 attempts. He then scored with each of his remaining m attempts during the second half of the game. If he scored on 90% of his shots taken, what is the value of m?

a. 10
b. 20
c. 30
d. 40

350. In the year 1900, the concentration of carbon dioxide (CO_2) in the atmosphere was approximately 280 parts per million. Currently, the CO_2 in the atmosphere is approximately 350 parts per million. What is the percent increase in CO_2 from 1900 until now?

a. 80%
b. 1.25%
c. .8%
d. 25%

351. The price for monthly monitoring services was decreased from $30 to $24. Calculate the percent decrease in the monthly charge for this service.

a. 20%

b. 25%

c. 30%

d. 35%

352. After spending $1,500 on a computer system in March, Jen finds out that her friend Janice bought the same exact system in April for 15% less. How much did Janice pay for her system?

a. $1500 + .15(1500)$

b. $.85(1500)$

c. $.15(1500)$

d. none of the above

353. One-quarter of a bag of coffee beans was consumed in three hours. What percent of coffee beans remains?

a. $\frac{3}{4}$%

b. 25%

c. 50%

d. 75%

354. How much water must be added to 2L of a 20% bleach–80% water mixture to yield a 10% bleach–90% water mixture?

a. 1 L

b. 2 L

c. 3 L

d. 4 L

355. What is the percent decrease when going from 180 to 60?

a. 200%

b. $133\frac{1}{3}$%

c. 80%

d. $66\frac{2}{3}$%

356. Frankie is about to use a 2-gallon cleaning solution consisting of 30% bleach and 70% water. He decides that it needs more bleach and adds an additional half-gallon of bleach. What are the percentages for this new solution?

a. 44% bleach–56% water

b. 40% bleach–60% water

c. 56% bleach–44% water

d. 60% bleach–44% water

S·E·C·T·I·O·N

ALGEBRA

5

There are many faces of algebra. You can interpret a sentence and translate it into algebra. You can take an algebraic expression and turn it into words. You may get a "Solve for x" question, or a "Simplify the equation" question. More advanced questions require FOIL or simultaneous equations. These seven sets introduce you to all the faces of algebra—which won't turn out to be so ugly after all.

SET 24

357. The statement, Cassie is seven years older than Elijah, can be expressed as
 a. $C + 7 = E$
 b. $E + 7 = C$
 c. $E - 7 = C$
 d. $E \div 7 = C$

358. 15 more than a number is 52. What is the number?
 a. 37
 b. 47
 c. 57
 d. 67

359. 6 less than 6 times a number is equal to 5 times one more than the number. What is the number?
 a. 0
 b. 7
 c. 11
 d. 13

360. A number is tripled and then decreased by 23 resulting in a value of 28. What was the original number?
 a. 69
 b. 40
 c. 25
 d. 17

361. The coordinator of a raffle gives out a tickets to b people and has c tickets left over. How many tickets were there initially?
 a. $a + c$
 b. $ab + c$
 c. $ab - c$
 d. $b + c$

362. Which of the statements below represents the expression $3x + 15 = 32$?
 a. 15 less than 3 times a number is 32.
 b. 32 times 3 is equal to 15 more than a number.
 c. 15 more than 3 times a number is 32.
 d. 3 more than 15 times a number is 32.

363. If an office needs to purchase x desks for D dollars, y chairs for E dollars, and z file cabinets for F dollars, which expression can be used to calculate the total cost, T?
 a. $T = xF + yE + zD$
 b. $T = xE + yD + zF$
 c. $T = xD + yE + zF$
 d. $T = xF + yE + zD$

364. Which expression best represents the following statement? *When a first number is added to the reciprocal of a different number, the result is a third number.*
 a. $1 + \frac{1}{b} = c$
 b. $a + \frac{1}{b} = c$
 c. $\frac{1}{a} + b = c$
 d. $a + \frac{1}{b} = 3$

365. Which expression represents $\frac{1}{2}$ added to the reciprocal of $\frac{2}{a}$?
 a. $\frac{a+1}{2}$
 b. $\frac{1}{2} + \frac{2}{a}$
 c. $-\frac{2}{a} + \frac{1}{2}$
 d. $\frac{2}{1} + \frac{a}{2}$

SET 25

366. Which of the following statements means the same as $3x - 8 = 25$?

  a. Three less than eight times a number is 25.

  b. Eight more than three times a number is 25.

  c. Three more than eight times a number is 25.

  d. Eight less than three times a number is 25.

367. Eight times one-third of a number is thirty-two. What is the number?

  a. 12

  b. $8\frac{2}{3}$

  c. $4\frac{1}{3}$

  d. $\frac{1}{3}$

368. When 42 is subtracted from a number, the result is 56. What is the number?

  a. 14

  b. 28

  c. 54

  d. 98

369. A number is decreased by 5 and then decreased by 13, resulting in 41. What was the original number?

  a. 23

  b. 59

  c. 62

  d. 70

370. The sum of 3 consecutive odd integers is 99. What is the middle number?

  a. 35

  b. 31

  c. 37

  d. 33

371. 30% of a number added to itself yields 156. What is the number?

  a. 120

  b. 50.03

  c. 520

  d. 550

372. $\frac{7}{8}$ of nine times a number is equal to ten times the number minus 17. Find the number.

  a. 18.6

  b. 8

  c. 1.86

  d. .32

373. Ten times 40% of a number is equal to 4 less than the product of 6 times the number. Find the number.

  a. 12

  b. 8

  c. 4

  d. 2

374. When three is added to the product of two and a number, the result is equivalent to 103 minus twice the number. Find the number.

  a. 25

  b. 14.7

  c. 1.47

  d. .25

375. If the sum of two numbers is 63, and the difference between the two numbers is 15, what is the smaller number?

  a. 48

  b. 39

  c. 24

  d. 18

376. What is the sum of $11x - 3y$ and $11y - 6x$?

   a. $17x + 8y$

   b. $5x + 8y$

   c. $5x + 14y$

   d. $5x - 9y$

SET 26

377. $x^2 - 8x$ is equivalent to

   a. $-x(x + 8)$

   b. $x(x - 8)$

   c. $x(x + 8)$

   d. $x(-x - 8)$

378. $8x^2y^3z^5 \div 2x$ is equal to

   a. $4x^2y^3z^5$

   b. $\frac{8x^2y^3z^5}{2}$

   c. $4xy^2z^5$

   d. $4xy^3z^5$

379. $x(2x^3 + 3y)$ can be expressed as

   a. $2x^4 + 3xy$

   b. $2x^3 + 3xy$

   c. $2x^4 + 3y$

   d. $x^4 + xy$

380. $2x(5x^2 + 3y)$ is equivalent to

   a. $5x^3 + 6xy$

   b. $10x^2 + 6xy$

   c. $10x^3 + 6xy$

   d. $10x^3 + 6y$

381. Simplify the following polynomial: $\frac{3x^2 + 3x}{3x^2 + 12}$

   a. $\frac{3x(x + 1)}{(x^2 + 3)}$

   b. $\frac{3x(x + 1)}{(x^2 + 4)}$

   c. $\frac{x(x + 1)}{(x^2 + 12)}$

   d. $\frac{x(x + 1)}{(x^2 + 4)}$

382. $(3a^4b^5)^2(a^2b)$ is equivalent to

   a. $3a^{10}b^{11}$

   b. $9a^{10}b^{11}$

   c. $9a^8b^8$

   d. $3a^8b^8$

383. If $PV = nRT$, which of the following represents a valid equation for T?

   a. $T = \frac{PV}{nR}$

   b. $PVnR = T$

   c. $\frac{PVR}{n} = T$

   d. $T = \frac{1}{PV} \times nR$

Use the following equations to answer questions 384 and 385.

$$\text{I. } E = \frac{F}{q} \qquad \text{II. } V = Er \qquad \text{III. } E = \frac{kQ}{r^2}$$

384. By combining two of the above equations, an equivalent expression for V would be

   a. $V = \frac{kQ}{r^2}$

   b. $V = QkR$

   c. $V = \frac{kQ}{r}$

   d. $V = kQ - r^2$

385. By combining two of the above equations, which of the following choices represents an equation for F?

   a. $F = Qqr^2$

   b. $F = \frac{kQ}{q}$

   c. $F = \frac{kQ}{r^2}$

   d. $F = \frac{kQ}{r^2} \cdot q$

386. For which values of x will the following number sentence *always* hold true? $5x + 15 \geq 10$

a. $x < -1$

b. $x \geq -1$

c. $x \geq 1$

d. $x < 1$

387. Which value below will make this number sentence true? $2x + 37 \geq 63$

a. -13

b. 5

c. 12

d. 13

388. For which value does the following inequality hold true? $5x - 27 \leq 43$

a. 13

b. 15

c. 17

d. 19

389. What is the solution for $5x < 23$?

a. $x < 115$

b. $x < 23$

c. $x < 4\frac{3}{5}$

d. $x > 23$

390. Solve for A: $B = \frac{C + A}{D - A}$

a. $A = \frac{BD - C}{1 + B}$

b. $A = \frac{D - C}{1 + B}$

c. $A = \frac{B - C}{C + B}$

d. $A = \frac{B + D}{C + B}$

SET 27

391. Solve for p: $2p + 5p - p = 3p + 19 + 8$

a. 9

b. 8.3

c. 3.38

d. 3

392. Solve for m: $1.25m + 7 = 17$

a. 12.5

b. 8

c. 4.5

d. 4

393. If $12x + 2y = 80$, and $x = 6$, what is the value of y?

a. -8

b. -4

c. 4

d. 8

394. Solve for x: $\frac{3x}{10} = \frac{15}{25}$

a. 2

b. 2.5

c. 3

d. 3.5

395. What is the value of x if $\frac{1}{4}x - 6 = 14$?

a. 5

b. 40

c. 60

d. 80

396. If $x > 40$, and x is prime, then x could be

a. 47

b. 51

c. 54

d. 55

397. If $x - 5 = 31$, then x is equal to
   a. 26
   b. 36
   c. 42
   d. 52

398. Solve for x: $14x + 23 = 65$
   a. 6.29
   b. 5.2
   c. 4
   d. 3

399. If $\frac{1}{9} = \frac{x}{63}$, what is the value of x?
   a. 9
   b. 7
   c. 6
   d. 5

400. Solve for x: $5x + 3 - 3x = 33 + x$
   a. 10
   b. 15
   c. 30
   d. 45

401. Solve for x: $\frac{1}{5}x + 11 = 14$
   a. $\frac{3}{5}$
   b. 2
   c. 15
   d. 25

402. Given $\frac{x}{2} + \frac{x}{8} = 15$, what is the value of x?
   a. $\frac{15}{8}$
   b. $14\frac{1}{8}$
   c. 24
   d. 30

403. Five crates weighing 85 lbs., 70 lbs., 92 lbs., 105 lbs., and x lbs. need to be delivered. If the average weight of the crates is 81 lbs., what is the value of x?
   a. 53 lbs.
   b. 61 lbs.
   c. 81 lbs.
   d. 88 lbs.

404. Use the following expression to solve for x:
$2x - 1 + 3x + 5 = 7x + 13$
   a. -4.5
   b. -3
   c. 3
   d. 6.5

405. What is the value of $x^2 + x - 6$ when $x = -3$?
   a. 6
   b. 3
   c. 2
   d. 0

SET 28

406. If $y = 3x - 13$, what is the value of x when $y = 26$?
   a. 13
   b. $8\frac{1}{3}$
   c. $4\frac{1}{3}$
   d. 3

407. What is the value of x, when $y = 2$ and $x = 13 - 4y$?
   a. 7
   b. 6
   c. 5
   d. 4

408. To calculate a temperature in Kelvin, we use the formula $K = C + 273$, where K = the temperature in Kelvin, and C = degrees in Celsius. If the temperature is 37° C, what is the temperature in Kelvin?

a. 217
b. 236
c. 301
d. 310

409. If $m = n(10 - 3) + (15 - n)$, solve for m when $n = 3$.

a. 36
b. 33
c. 30
d. 27

410. If $a = 21$, $b = 2$, and $c = -3$, what is the value of $\frac{2a - bc}{3}$

a. 16
b. 14
c. 12
d. 10

411. Given $y = 12z - (10 + z)$, solve for y when $z = 5$.

a. 30
b. 45
c. 60
d. 75

412. If $\frac{a}{(b - 1)} = 23$, what is the value of $\frac{3a}{(3b - 3)} + 7$?

a. $23 + \frac{3a}{(3b)}$
b. 16
c. $(b - 1)(23)(7)$
d. 30

413. If $x + y = 5$, what is the numerical equivalent of $7y + 6x - 6y - 5x + 15$?

a. 15
b. 20
c. 25
d. 30

414. Evan jogs past Ralph's house at 8:12 A.M. He continues onward at the same pace and passes Joe's house at 9:42 A.M. If Joe lives 8 miles away from Ralph, how fast does Evan jog per hour?

a. 4 mph.
b. 5 mph.
c. $5\frac{1}{3}$ mph.
d. $6\frac{2}{3}$ mph.

415. Erik and James fixed 55 computers during the course of the weekend. If James fixed 5 less than $\frac{2}{3}$ of Erik's total, how many computers did Erik fix?

a. 36
b. 34
c. 19
d. 16

416. Lars uses the formula $\frac{T}{5} = m$ to approximate how far away (in miles) lightning is striking. T represents the amount of time (in seconds) between a flash of lightning and a flash of thunder. If Lars sees lightning and counts 15 seconds before hearing thunder, approximately how many miles, m, away from Lars, did the lightning strike?

a. $\frac{1}{3}$ mi.
b. $\frac{2}{3}$ mi.
c. 3 mi.
d. 6 mi.

417. Harry can unload 80 boxes in a half hour and Keith can unload 120 boxes in an hour. How long will Keith have to work in order to unload the same number of boxes as Harry can unload in one hour?

a. 1 hr. $\frac{1}{3}$ min.
b. 1 hr. 15 min.
c. 1 hr. 18 min.
d. 1 hr. 20 min.

418. In a study group, the ratio of men to women is 3:4. If there are 21 people in the group, how many men are there?

a. 3
b. 6
c. 9
d. 12

419. There was a 5:1 ratio of men to women in a karate class. Then, seven women joined the class resulting in the current 3:2 male to female ratio. What is the total number of *people* currently enrolled in the karate class?

a. 3
b. 10
c. 18
d. 25

420. How many pounds of raisins, costing $1.25 per pound, must be mixed with 5 lbs. of nuts, costing $8 per pound, in order to create a mixture that costs $5 per pound?

a. 9 lbs.
b. 4.5 lbs.
c. 4 lbs.
d. 3.5 lbs.

SET 29

421. If $2x + y = 13$, and $5x - y = 1$, what is the value of x?

a. -2
b. 1
c. 2
d. 3

422. If $5x + 3y = 20$, and $x - y = 4$, what is the value of $x + y$?

a. 4
b. 8
c. 12
d. It cannot be determined based on the information given.

423. Find the product of $(x + 8)$ and $(x - 7)$.

a. $x^2 + x + 15$
b. $x^2 - x - 15$
c. $x^2 + x - 56$
d. $x^2 + x + 56$

424. If $3x + y = 40$ and $x - 2y = 4$, what is the value of y?

a. $-5\frac{3}{5}$
b. 4
c. $5\frac{3}{5}$
d. 8

425. What is the solution to $x^2 + 12x - 13 = 0$?

a. $x = -13$ and -1
b. $x = -13$ and 1
c. $x = 13$ and -4
d. $x = 5$ and 7

426. Solve for x: $x^2 - 2x = 24$

a. $x = -4, 6$
b. $x = -6, 4$
c. $x = -2, 6$
d. $x = -6, 2$

427. Solve for x: $2x^2 - x - 1 = 0$
   a. $1, -1$
   b. $-\frac{1}{2}, 1$
   c. $-1, \frac{1}{2}$
   d. $2, -1$

428. Which answer mathematically expresses the product of five more than x and 1 more than twice x?
   a. $x^2 + 11x + 5$
   b. $2x^2 + x + 5$
   c. $2x^2 + 10x + 5$
   d. $2x^2 + 11x + 5$

429. A number, n, can be described as follows: Five plus a number is multiplied by 3 less than the number. Solving which of the following equations will yield the correct values for n?
   a. $5n \times 3n$
   b. $n + 5 \times n - 3$
   c. $(n + 5)(3 - n)$
   d. $n^2 + 2n - 15$

430. Simplify the following expression:
   $(5x + 1)(2y + 2) = 10xy + 12$
   a. $10x + 2y + 2 = 10$
   b. $10x + y = 10$
   c. $5x + y = 5$
   d. $5x - y = 5$

431. Given that N is a composite number, solve the following: One more than the number N is multiplied by N, resulting in a value that is equal to 9 times N minus 12. Find N.
   a. 2 only
   b. 6 only
   c. 2 and 6
   d. -6 only

432. Which of the choices below equals the following equation? $\frac{x-3}{2x} \div \frac{x^2-9}{6x}$
   a. $\frac{x^2-1}{2x}$
   b. $\frac{3}{x+3}$
   c. $\frac{3+x}{x+3}$
   d. $\frac{x^2-1}{3x}$

433. Which of the following is equivalent to $(x^2 - x - 6) \div (x - 3)$?
   a. $x + 2$
   b. $x - 3$
   c. $x^2 - 3$
   d. $x^2 + 2$

SET 30

434. $\frac{x^2 + 9x + 14}{x^2 - 4}$ is equivalent to which of the following expressions?
   a. $\frac{x-7}{x-2}$
   b. $\frac{x+7}{x-2}$
   c. $\frac{x+7}{x+2}$
   d. $\frac{x-7}{x+2}$

435. For all $x \neq \pm 4$, $\frac{x^2 + 2x - 8}{x^2 - 16}$ is equivalent to
   a. $\frac{x-2}{x-4}$
   b. $\frac{x+2}{x+4}$
   c. $\frac{x-2}{x+4}$
   d. $\frac{x+2}{x-4}$

436. The quotient of $x^2 + 4x + 4$ and $x + 2$ is
   a. $x - 2$
   b. $x + 2$
   c. $x^2 + 2x$
   d. $x^2 - 2x$

437. Train A and Train B are 210 miles apart and heading towards each other on adjacent tracks. If Train A travels at 70 mph., and Train B travels at 50 mph., how long will it take until the trains pass each other?

a. 1 hr.

b. 1 hr. 30 min.

c. 1 hr. 45 min.

d. 2 hrs.

438. The ratio of math majors to English majors to chemistry majors is 3:2:1. If there are 12,000 students attaining these majors, how many are English students?

a. 2,000

b. 3,000

c. 4,000

d. 5,000

439. During a film festival, non-students must pay $11.75 to view a double feature. Students receive a discounted rate and pay $6.75. Which of the following expressions can be used to calculate the amount collected from 75 non-students and 30 students?

a. $75(11.75) + 30(6.75)$

b. $75(6.75) + 30(11.75)$

c. $(75 + 30)(6.75 + 11.75)$

d. $75 + 30 \times 6.75 \times 11.75$

440. If Deirdre walks from Point A to Point B to Point C at a constant rate of 2 mph. without stopping, what is the total time she takes?

a. $(x + y) \times 2$

b. $2x + 2y$

c. $xy \div 2$

d. $(x + y) \div 2$

441. If $5x - 5y = 60$, what is the value of $x - y$?

a. 0

b. 10

c. 12

d. 15

442. If $4x + 8y + 2x - 2y = 48$, what is the value of $x + y$?

a. 6

b. 8

c. 12

d. 14

S·E·C·T·I·O·N

GEOMETRY 6

The final eight sets in this book all pertain to geometry and measurement. You'll review terminology, area formulas, perimeter and circumference, volume, parallel lines, and surface area, as well as deal with all the shapes you expected to see (circles, squares, triangles, and so forth). Be sure to consult the chart in the introductory section when prepping for a particular test, so that you will focus on the appropriate sets.

SET 31

443. What is the area of the square below?

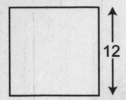

a. 48
b. 60
c. 84
d. 144

444. A circular fountain has a diameter of 15 feet, as shown below. What is its radius?

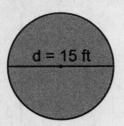

a. 30 ft.
b. 225π ft.²
c. 7.5 ft.
d. 15π

445. One side of a regular hexagon is 4 inches long. What is the perimeter of the hexagon?
a. 16 in.
b. 18 in.
c. 20 in.
d. 24 in.

446. What is the area of the circle below?

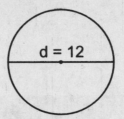

a. 144π
b. 36π
c. 12π
d. 6π

447. Which pair of angles are adjacent?

a. A and C
b. B and D
c. A and B
d. C and E

448. What is the perimeter of the square below?

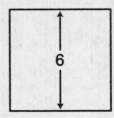

a. 24
b. 36
c. 40
d. 48

449. In the diagram below, ABCD is a trapezoid. Which answer choice represents a pair of parallel sides?

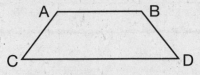

- **a.** $\overline{AB}$ and $\overline{BD}$
- **b.** $\overline{AB}$ and $\overline{CD}$
- **c.** $\overline{AC}$ and $\overline{BD}$
- **d.** $\overline{CD}$ and $\overline{AC}$

450. If the area of circle X is 25π, what is its circumference?

- **a.** 5π
- **b.** 10π
- **c.** 15π
- **d.** 20π

451. Which choice represents a pair of perpendicular line segments?

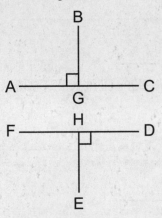

- **a.** $\overline{AC}$ and $\overline{FD}$
- **b.** $\overline{BG}$ and $\overline{AC}$
- **c.** $\overline{BG}$ and $\overline{HE}$
- **d.** $\overline{AG}$ and $\overline{HD}$

452. Which of the following statements regarding angles *a*, *b*, *c*, and *d* below is true?

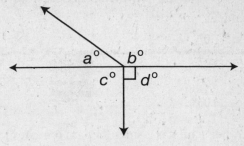

- **a.** *a* & *c* are complementary
- **b.** *d* & *b* are both right angles
- **c.** *a* & *b* are supplementary
- **d.** *c* & *b* are both obtuse angles

453. Below is a pair of similar triangles. What is the length of $\overline{FG}$?

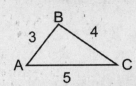

Note: Figure not drawn to scale.

- **a.** 6
- **b.** 8
- **c.** 10
- **d.** 12

454. What is the area of the right triangle below?

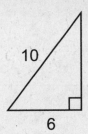

- **a.** 8
- **b.** 16
- **c.** 24
- **d.** 32

SET 32

455. Which of the following angles is an obtuse angle?

a. 60°

b. 85°

c. 90°

d. 105°

456. A hexagon has 2 sides that are 6 inches long. If the remaining sides are all 4 inches long, what does the perimeter of the hexagon equal?

a. 2 + 2 + 6 + 6 + 6+ 6

b. 6 + 6 + 4 + 4 + 4+ 4

c. 6 + 6 + 4 + 4 + 4+ 4 + 4 + 4

d. 2 + 2 + 6 + 6 + 6+ 6 + 4 + 4

457. In the figure below, which of the following is a right angle?

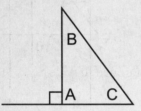

a. A

b. B

c. C

d. D

458. An isosceles triangle has

a. two complementary angles.

b. two congruent sides.

c. two supplementary angles.

d. two obtuse sides.

459. Which of the following is an acute angle?

a. 75°

b. 90°

c. 105°

d. 180°

460. How many feet of fence are needed to surround the rectangular area below?

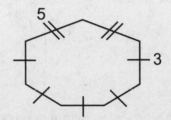

a. 1104 ft.

b. 545 ft.

c. 142 ft.

d. 94 ft.

461. What is the perimeter of the polygon below?

a. 15

b. 20

c. 25

d. 30

462. What is the area of a circle with a diameter of 8 inches?

a. 8π in.^{2}

b. 16π in.^{2}

c. 32π in.^{2}

d. 64π in.^{2}

463. How much larger is the area of Circle B than the area of Circle A?

Circle A

Circle B

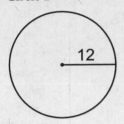

- a. 144π
- b. 108π
- c. 72π
- d. 48π

464. Which figures represent regular polygons?

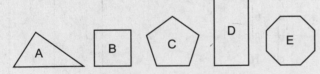

- a. A, B, and C
- b. B, C, and D
- c. B, C, and E
- d. A, D, and E

465. The length of a rectangle is 8. If its width is half its length, what will its area equal?

- a. $2 \times \frac{1}{2} \times 8$
- b. $\frac{1}{2} \times 8 \times \frac{1}{2} \times 8$
- c. $8 + \frac{1}{2} \times 8$
- d. $8 \times \frac{1}{2}(8)$

466. What is the perimeter of the polygon below?

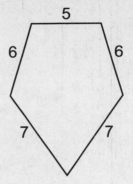

- a. 31
- b. 37
- c. 41
- d. 47

467. Which 3 angles will add up to form a straight line?

- a. 90°, 60°, 20°
- b. 30°, 20°, 40°
- c. 91°, 65°, 24°
- d. 50°, 50°, 50°

468. The complementary angle to 42° is

- a. 138°
- b. 58°
- c. 48°
- d. 30°

SET 33

469. What is the area of the trapezoid below?

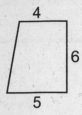

- a. 15
- b. 22
- c. 27
- d. 30

470. If the width of the rectangle below is doubled, what happens to its area?

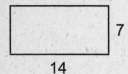

- a. it is halved
- b. it is doubled
- c. it is multiplied by 4
- d. it is multiplied by $\frac{1}{4}$

471. What is the surface area of a closed box with dimensions 5 cm × 7 cm × 4 cm?

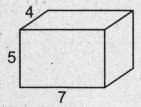

- a. 166 cm²
- b. 140 cm²
- c. 100 cm²
- d. 83 cm²

472. Figure OPQR is a square with side = 7 that has been sliced into 8 equal triangles as shown below. What is the area of the shaded region?

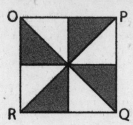

- a. 20
- b. 24.5
- c. 32
- d. 49

473. What is the length, L, of the rectangle below?

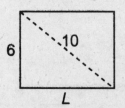

- a. 6
- b. 8
- c. 10
- d. 12

474. What is the perimeter of the triangle below?

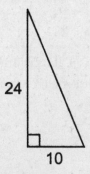

- a. 60
- b. 57
- c. 37
- d. 26

475. What is the area of the trapezoid below?

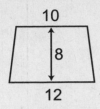

a. 120
b. 108
c. 88
d. 80

476. If the side of the square below is doubled, what happens to its area?

a. it is halved
b. it is doubled
c. it is multiplied by $\frac{1}{4}$
d. it is quadrupled

477. HIJK (below) is a square. Given that $\overline{HK} = 4$ units, what is the area of the shaded region?

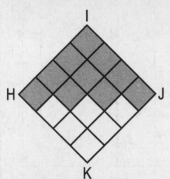

a. $\frac{1}{10}$ square units
b. $\frac{10}{16}$ square units
c. 10 square units
d. 16 square units

478. If ΔABC is similar to ΔXYZ, which of the following is *false*?

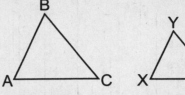

a. $\frac{AB}{XY} = \frac{BC}{YZ}$
b. $\frac{BC}{YZ} = \frac{AC}{XZ}$
c. $\frac{AB}{XY} = \frac{AC}{XZ}$
d. $\frac{AC}{XZ} = \frac{AB}{YZ}$

479. A light shines 15 feet in all directions. What is the area illuminated by the light?

a. 15π
b. 30π
c. 100π
d. 225π

480. Analyze the 2 triangles below to determine which of the following statements is *true*.

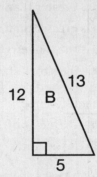

a. Triangle A and Triangle B are similar.
b. The numerical value of the perimeter of Triangle A equals the numerical value of its area.
c. The numerical value of the perimeter of Triangle B equals the numerical value of its area.
d. Triangle A and Triangle B are congruent.

481. How many 4″ × 4″ tiles are needed to cover a floor that is 4′ × 3′?

   a. 108 tiles

   b. 100 tiles

   c. 64 tiles

   d. 48 tiles

482. The perimeter of a four-sided lot is 32 yards. What is the greatest possible area of the lot?

   a. 60 yd.^{2}

   b. 63 yd.^{2}

   c. 64 yd.^{2}

   d. 66 yd.^{2}

483. Which statement is true regarding the figure below?

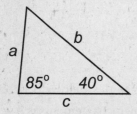

   a. Side b is greater than sides $a + c$.

   b. Side a is greater than side c.

   c. Side b is the longest.

   d. Side c is the shortest.

484. What is the difference in the distance around a circle with a diameter of 14, and a square with a side of 6? Use $\frac{22}{7}$ for π.

   a. 8

   b. 20

   c. 80

   d. 118

485. What is the area of the figure below?

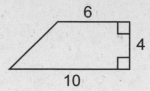

   a. 24

   b. 32

   c. 46

   d. 64

486. △ABC is similar to △DEF. What is the length of $\overline{EF}$?

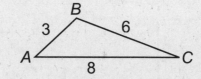

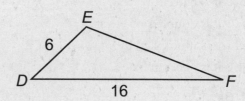

   a. 12

   b. 14

   c. 18

   d. 20

SET 34

487. A 13-foot plank of wood is leaning against the side of a building. If the top of the plank is 12 feet from the ground, how far is the bottom of the plank from the wall?

a. 5 feet

b. 6 feet

c. 8 feet

d. 10 feet

488. A wedge is removed from a metal disc as shown below. What is the area that remains?

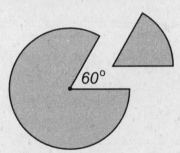

r = 12

a. 144π

b. 130π

c. 120π

d. 24π

489. If it costs 75¢ per square yard to lacquer a wood surface, how much would it cost to lacquer a wood floor that is 9 feet by 15 feet?

a. $10,125

b. $101.25

c. $20.25

d. $11.25

490. In the diagram below, what is the area of the deck (shown in gray)?

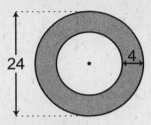

a. 144π ft.²

b. 108π ft.²

c. 92π ft.²

d. 80π ft.²

491. LMNO is a square with side = 8. If $\overline{OM}$ bisects $\overline{LN}$, what is the area of the shaded region?

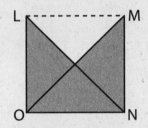

a. 16

b. 32

c. 48

d. 64

492. If the 2 shortest sides of a rectangle add up to 24 feet, and its perimeter is 64 feet, what is the longest side of the rectangle?

a. 12

b. 14

c. 20

d. 24

493. If ABCD is a square with side = 14, what is the area of the shaded region?

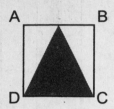

a. 196
b. 98
c. 80
d. 64

494. If Circle Q has been divided into 3 equal sections, what is the area of the shaded region, given $r = 6$?

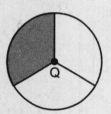

a. 12π
b. 24π
c. 36π
d. 48π

495. If the area of the triangle below is 40, what is its height, h?

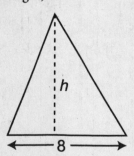

a. 5
b. 10
c. 15
d. 20

496. If the average of a and b is 7, what is the area of the trapezoid shown below?

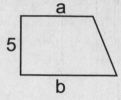

a. 35
b. 70
c. 80
d. It cannot be determined by the information given.

497. What is the perimeter of the triangle below?

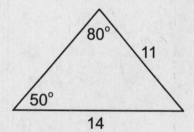

a. 11
b. 25
c. 36
d. It cannot be determined based on the information given.

498. A circle is inscribed inside square ABCD. If the area of square ABCD is 4, what is the area of the shaded region?

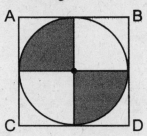

   a. 4
   b. $3\frac{3}{4}\pi$
   c. 2
   d. $\frac{1}{2}\pi$

499. What is the area of the parallelogram below?

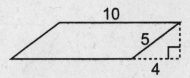

   a. 50
   b. 40
   c. 30
   d. 20

500. A rectangle with a length twice its width has a perimeter, P, of 132. What is the length of the rectangle?

   a. 44
   b. 30
   c. 22
   d. 14

501. A rectangular container that is 3 feet by 2 feet by 8 inches is to be filled with water. How many cubic feet of water will it fill completely?

   a. 48 ft.³
   b. 24 ft.³
   c. 8 ft.³
   d. 4 ft.³

SET 35

502. Given the rectangle ABCD below, what is the sum of $r° + s°$?

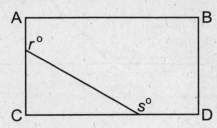

   a. 90°
   b. 180°
   c. 270°
   d. 310°

503. Which point is located at $(-7, -2)$?

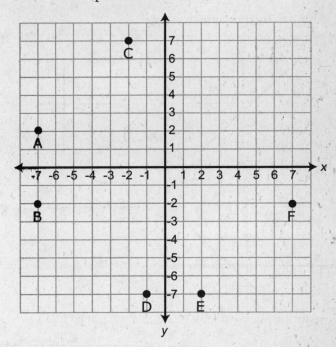

   a. A
   b. B
   c. C
   d. D

504. In the figure below, if $\overline{AB}$, $\overline{CD}$, and $\overline{EF}$ are parallel, what is the value of *y*?

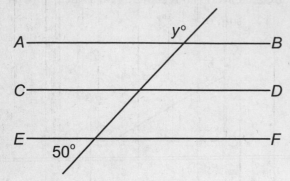

a. 50
b. 60
c. 130
d. 140

505. Which statement is true?

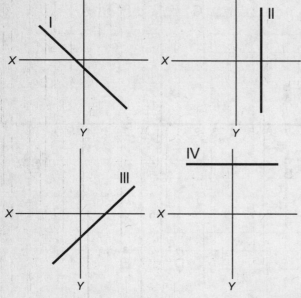

a. Line I has zero slope.
b. Line II has no slope.
c. Line III has a negative slope.
d. Line IV has a negative slope.

506. If Sally makes $10/hr., which graph best represents her earnings?

a.
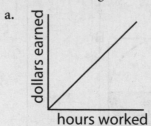

b.
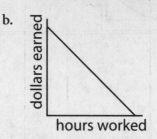

c.
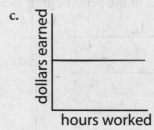

d.
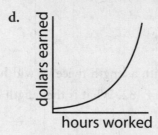

507. A line passes through points $(-2, 4)$ and $(7, 3)$. What is its slope?

a. $\frac{1}{9}$
b. $-\frac{1}{9}$
c. $\frac{7}{9}$
d. $-\frac{7}{9}$

508. If $\overline{AB}$ is parallel to $\overline{CD}$, what is the value of p?

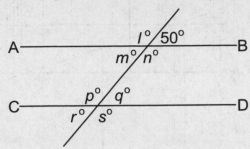

  a. 50
  b. 60
  c. 130
  d. 140

509. Which line is perpendicular to the line $y = -2x + 1$.
  a. $y = -2x + 9$
  b. $y = -\frac{1}{2}x + 1$
  c. $y = -4x + 1$
  d. $y = \frac{1}{2}x + 8$

510. If the slope of the line below is 2, what is the value of q?

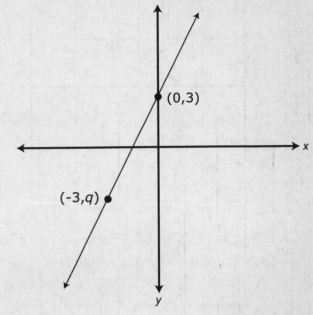

  a. -3
  b. 3
  c. -9
  d. 9

511. If $\overline{AE}$ is perpendicular to $\overline{DC}$, what is the value of x?

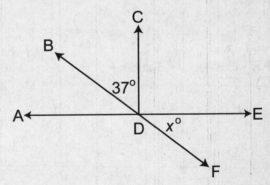

  a. 37
  b. 40
  c. 47
  d. 53

512. Lines $\overline{AB}$ and $\overline{CD}$ are parallel. What is the value of x?

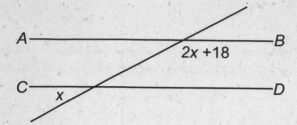

a. 18°
b. 36°
c. 54°
d. 62°

513. The graph of $2x - y + 8 = 0$ crosses the x-axis at which of the following coordinates?

a. $(0, 8)$
b. $(-4, 0)$
c. $(8, 0)$
d. $(0, -4)$

514. Which equation represents a line parallel to $y = 2x + 8$?

a. $y = \frac{1}{2}x + 8$
b. $y = 2x - 4$
c. $y = -2x + 8$
d. $y = -\frac{1}{2}x - 4$

515. The lines $y = 5$ and $y = x - 3$ intersect at point

a. $(5, 8)$
b. $(5, 2)$
c. $(2, 5)$
d. $(8, 5)$

516. Lines $\overline{LM}$ and $\overline{NO}$ are parallel. Solve for x.

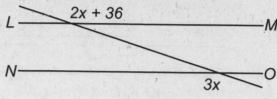

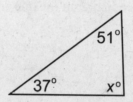

a. 36°
b. 24°
c. 18°
d. 12°

SET 36

517. What is the value of x?

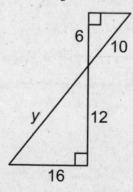

a. 37°
b. 51°
c. 63°
d. 92°

518. In the figure below, what is the value of y?

a. 15
b. 20
c. 30
d. 40

519. What is the perimeter of the triangle below?

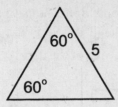

a. 12.5
b. 13
c. 15
d. 18

520. What is the perimeter of the triangle shown below?

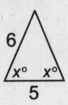

a. 11
b. 14
c. 15
d. 17

521. As the wheel pictured below travels 942 cm, how many revolutions does it make? (Use $\pi = 3.14$)

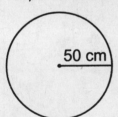

a. 5
b. 4
c. 3
d. 2

522. Which figure below has the greatest volume?

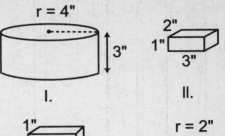

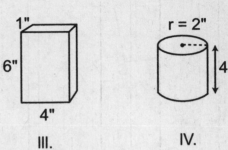

a. I
b. II
c. III
d. IV

523. *ABCD* is a square. What is the value of *x*?

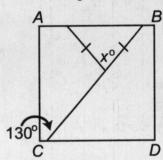

a. 50
b. 65
c. 80
d. 85

524. What is the distance between $(1, -1)$ and $(7, 7)$?

a. 6
b. 7
c. 9
d. 10

525. If the perimeter of the figure below is 67, what is the length of side $\overline{DE}$?

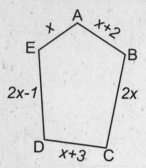

a. 7
b. 9
c. 12
d. 17

526. What is the area of the shaded region below?

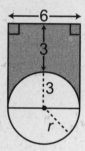

Note: Figure not drawn to scale.

a. $36 - 9\pi$
b. $36 - 4.5\pi$
c. $18 - 9\pi$
d. $18 - 4.5\pi$

527. If $b = a + 2$, and the area of the rectangular piece of paper below is 28, what is the value of a?

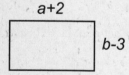

a. 5
b. -6
c. -6 or 5
d. -5 or 6

528. Christina wants to build a deck (shown in gray) around part of her house. If her house is represented by the square with side = 22 ft. (shown in white), what is the area of the deck?

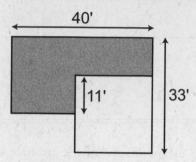

a. 1,320 ft.^{2}
b. 638 ft.^{2}
c. 440 ft.^{2}
d. 198 ft.^{2}

529. The cylindrical can below has a label that wraps around the entire can with no overlap. Calculate the area of the label using $\pi = \frac{22}{7}$.

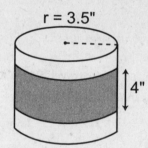

a. 14 in.^{2}
b. 22 in.^{2}
c. 88 in.^{2}
d. 100 in.^{2}

530. What is the base of a triangle with a height of 8 and an area of 28?

a. 6
b. 7
c. 8
d. 9

531. Two sides of a triangle are 21 inches and 23 inches, respectively. Which of the following cannot be the length of the third side?

   a. 21.54 in.

   b. 22 in.

   c. 43.5 in.

   d. 44 in.

532. If x is equal to 6, what is the distance of $\overline{AB}$ below?

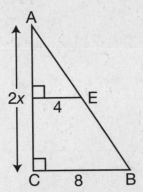

   a. 10

   b. $2\sqrt{52}$

   c. 20

   d. $7\sqrt{3}$

SET 37

533. The cylindrical tank pictured below needs to be filled with water up to a height of 4 feet. How many gallons of water must be added to the empty tank if 1 ft.³ contains 7.5 gallons of water? (Use $\pi = 3.14$)

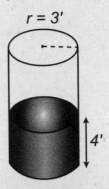

   a. 113.04 gallons

   b. 248.6 gallons

   c. 716 gallons

   d. 847.8 gallons

534. The section of lawn pictured below is a perfect circle, and Maynard needs to cover the area with sand before installing his pool. If one bag of sand covers $52\frac{1}{3}$ ft.² and costs \$7.50, how much money does he have to spend on sand?

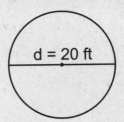

   a. \$45.00

   b. \$50.25

   c. \$92.75

   d. \$180.00

535. If cast iron weighs approximately .25 lb. per cubic inch, how much would the cylinder shown below weigh? (Use $\frac{22}{7}$ for π.)

r =1 in.

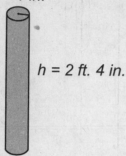

h = 2 ft. 4 in.

a. 7 lbs.
b. 16 lbs.
c. 22 lbs.
d. 32 lbs.

536. If r = 4, what is the volume of the sphere below?

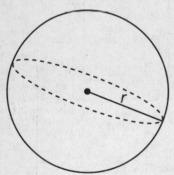

a. $21\frac{1}{3}\pi$
b. $42\frac{1}{3}\pi$
c. $85\frac{1}{3}\pi$
d. 98π

537. What is the volume of the cone below?

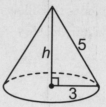

a. 12π
b. 18π
c. 24π
d. 28π

538. What is the volume of the pyramid below if its height is 4 cm?

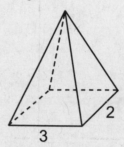

a. 8 cm^3
b. 16 cm^3
c. 24 cm^3
d. 30 cm^3

539. What is the area of a circle, whose center is at (−1, 3) and that passes through (3, 3)?

a. 4π
b. 8π
c. 16π
d. 64π

540. A circle with center (1, 1) passes through the point (−2, 5). What is its diameter?

a. 5
b. 10
c. 12
d. 14

SET 38

Reference Information for questions 541-545:

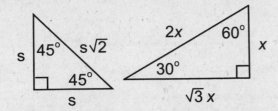

541. What is the value of *k* in the figure below?

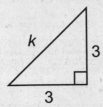

a. 9
b. 6
c. $3\sqrt{2}$
d. $5\sqrt{3}$

542. What is the value of *m* in the figure below?

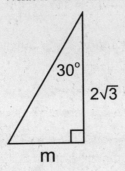

a. 2
b. 3
c. $2\sqrt{3}$
d. $3\sqrt{3}$

543. What is the height, *h*, of the triangle below?

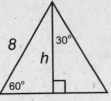

a. $8\sqrt{3}$
b. $4\sqrt{3}$
c. 8
d. 4

544. If the radius of the circle below is 19, what is the value of *w*?

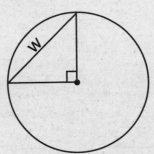

a. 19
b. $19\sqrt{2}$
c. 9.5
d. 38

545. If the perimeter of the triangle below equals $18 + 9\sqrt{2}$, what is its area?

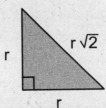

a. $6 + 2\sqrt{2}$
b. $16 + \sqrt{2}$
c. $40\frac{1}{2}$
d. $162\frac{1}{2}$

ANSWERS

SECTION 1—MISCELLANEOUS MATH

SET 1

1. b	18. a	35. c
2. c	19. c	36. d
3. a	20. d	37. a
4. b	21. a	38. c
5. a	22. c	39. b
6. d	23. c	40. c
7. c	24. a	41. d
8. b	25. d	42. a
9. d	26. d	43. b
10. c	27. b	44. c
11. b	28. a	45. a
12. a	29. c	46. b
13. d	30. b	47. d
14. b	31. a	48. c
15. c	32. d	49. a
16. b	33. b	50. b
17. d	34. c	

SET 2

51. b. 4! means 4 *factorial*, which is equivalent to $4 \times 3 \times 2 \times 1$.

52. d. To simplify $(-5)(-3)(2) - |-20|$, let's find the absolute value of -20. $|-20| = 20$ because the *absolute value* is just the *positive* distance from zero on the number line. Rewriting the question as $(-5)(-3)(2) - 20$ makes it appear less intimidating. Now we can multiply out the first part of this expression: $(-5)(-3)(2) = 30$. Note that multiplying a negative by a negative produced a positive. The whole expression becomes $30 - 20$, which equals 10.

53. a. When dealing with radicals, you can only combine terms if the roots are the same. So let's try to pull some numbers out from under the radical. $\sqrt{72} = \sqrt{36 \cdot 2}$, and because 6^2 is 36, we can pull a six out from under the radical. Thus, $\sqrt{72} = 6\sqrt{2}$. Now we will look at $\sqrt{200}$. $\sqrt{200} = \sqrt{2 \cdot 100}$, and because $10^2 = 100$, we can pull a ten out from under the radical. So, $\sqrt{200} = 10\sqrt{2}$. Now we are dealing with the same root, namely $\sqrt{2}$, so we can combine terms. $6\sqrt{2} + 10\sqrt{2} = 16\sqrt{2}$.

54. c. This question is testing your ability to deal with the order of operations. Remember that the order of operations is *Parentheses, Exponents, Multiplication, Division, Addition, Subtraction*. Some people remember this by saying "*Please excuse my dear Aunt Sally*," or simply *PEMDAS*. When tackling $121 - 2(11-8)^3$, we first deal with the parentheses: $121 - 2(3)^3$. Next, handle the exponent: $121 - 2(27)$. Third, multiply: $121 - 54$. Last, we subtract to get 67.

55. d. The question asks us for a number that is divisible by 7 and 5. This means that the answer must be able to be divided by both 7 and 5 with no remainders. Choice **a**, 28, is divisible by 7, but not by 5. Choice **b**, 40, is divisible by 5 only. Choice **c** is divisible by 7 only, and choice **d** is divisible by both 7 and 5, making it correct. Note $7 \times 15 = 105$ and $5 \times 21 = 105$.

56. d. Looking at 17,822, we see that the 1 is in the ten thousands place, the 7 is in the thousands place, the 8 is in the hundreds place, the 2 is in the tens place, and the 2 is in the units (ones) place. This is equivalent to $10000 + 7000 + 800 + 20 + 2$. Choice **d** represents this expression.

57. c. We need 4 consecutive even numbers whose sum is 44. Consecutive means that the numbers will be in order, and because we are told that we need consecutive *even* numbers, we are looking for even numbers that are in order and add to 44. Choice **a** contains odd numbers and is therefore wrong. Looking at choice **b**, we see that these are, in fact, consecutive even numbers. Do they add to 44? $4 + 6 + 8 + 10 = 28$. Nope! We try **c**: $8 + 10 + 12 + 14 = 44$. Thus, **c** is correct.

58. b. 12^3 is the same as $12 \cdot 12 \cdot 12$, or $12 \times 12 \times 12$, or $(12)(12)(12)$. These are three different ways of mathematically expressing 12 times 12 times 12. Thus, only choice **b** is correct.

59. c. First, solve for the value in the parentheses. Thus, $(12 \times 5) - 8$ becomes $60 - 8$. Next, we subtract to get 52.

60. b. $\sqrt{125}$ can be rewritten as $\sqrt{5 \cdot 25}$. Because $25 = 5^2$, we can pull a 5 out from under the radical sign. Thus, we have $5\sqrt{5}$, which is choice b. If you chose choice a, you found the cube root instead of the square root. $\sqrt[3]{125} = 5$. $\sqrt{125} = 5\sqrt{5}$.

61. d. 5^3 is another way of writing $5 \times 5 \times 5$ which equals $25 \times 5 = 125$.

62. a. $3\sqrt{32}$ can also be written as $3\sqrt{16 \cdot 2}$, because $16 \times 2 = 32$. Thus, choice a is correct. It would also be correct to pull a 4 out from under the radical sign (because $4^2 = 16$) to yield $3 \cdot 4\sqrt{2}$. This simplifies to $12\sqrt{2}$. However, neither of these correct equivalents is given as an answer choice.

63. b. In this case, it is easiest to use trial and error. We are looking for the answer choice, which, when squared, will result in 1151. Let's look at choice a: $29.7 \times 29.7 = 882.09$. Nope! So let's look at b: $33.9 \times 33.9 = 1149.21$. That is awfully close. Since 35×35 is 1225, we know that choice c will be even larger than this, and d will be way too large. Thus, we choose b.

64. c. $13 \times 13 \times 13 \times 13 \times 13$ is equivalent to 13 raised to the fifth power, or 13^5, choice c. Choice b, $13^2 + 13^3$, is not equivalent to 13^5. However, $13^2 \times 13^3 = 13^5$. Remember that when multiplying with the same base (in this case 13) you just add the exponents.

65. d. $\sqrt[3]{125}$ means that you are taking the *cube root* of 125. This means we are looking for a number that when cubed gives us the value of 125; $x \cdot x \cdot x = 125$. Here, x is 5. Note that -5 is not correct because $-5 \cdot -5 \cdot -5 = -125$.

66. b. We simply take the square root of the numerator (top) and denominator (bottom) of $\frac{1}{64}$. $\sqrt{1} = 1$ and $\sqrt{64} = 8$. Thus, $\sqrt{\frac{1}{64}} = \frac{1}{8}$.

67. d. Given $(-2)^3 + (-3)^2$, first we will cube the -2. Remember that a negative number raised to an odd power produces a *negative* value. $-2 \cdot -2 \cdot -2 = -8$. The question simplified to $-8 + (-3)^2$. We square the -3 to get 9. Remember that a negative number raised to an even power produces a *positive* value. Now we have $-8 + 9$, which equals 1.

68. c. If you are familiar with the squares of common numbers, you can recognize that $6^2 = 36$, $7^2 = 49$, and $8^2 = 64$. How would this help you? Well, you would know that choices a and b would be too small because their squares are less than 49. You would also know that choice d would be too large because its square would be over 64. Thus c is the correct choice.

69. a. $25^2 = 25 \cdot 25 = 625$. $21^2 = 21 \cdot 21 = 441$. We subtract: $625 - 441 = 184$.

70. d. Remember to follow the order of operations inside the absolute value walls. $|-16 \times -2 + 5 \times 8| = |32 + 40| = 72$. Notice that multiplication comes before addition in the order of operations: *Parentheses, Exponents, Multiplication, Division, Addition, Subtraction.*

SET 3

71. **b.** The question asks us for a number that is divisible by 8 and 6. This means that the answer must be able to be divided by 8 and 6 with no remainders. Choice **a**, 16, is divisible by 8, but not by 6. Choice **b**, 24, is divisible by both 8 and 6, so it is correct. Choice **c** is divisible by 8 only, and choice **d** is divisible by neither 6 nor 8.

72. **c.** Looking at 13,450, we see that the 1 is in the ten thousands place, the 3 is in the thousands place, the 4 is in the hundreds place, the 5 is in the tens place, and the 0 is in the units (ones) place. This is equivalent to $10,000 + 3,000 + 400 + 50 + 0$. Choice **c** represents this expression without adding the zero.

73. **a.** We need 4 consecutive odd numbers whose sum is 24. Consecutive means that the numbers will be in order, and because we are told that we need consecutive odd numbers, we are looking for odd numbers that are in order. Choices **b** and **c** contain even numbers and are, therefore, wrong. Looking at choice **a**, we see that these are, in fact, consecutive odd numbers. Do they add to 24? $3 + 5 + 7 + 9 = 24$. Thus, **a** is correct.

74. **d.** 6^3 is the same as $6 \times 6 \times 6$, but this is not a choice. However, choice **d** is equivalent: 36×6.

75. **b.** The square root of 64, or $\sqrt{64}$, is equal to 8 because $8^2 = 64$. Choice **a** represents the *cube root* of 64 and *not* the square root of 64. Choice **b**, $4\sqrt{4} = 4 \times 2 = 8$, and is therefore correct. Choice **c**, $4\sqrt{2} \neq 8$, and choice **d**, 8^2, is also not equal to 8.

76. **c.** First, you should list all factors of each of the given numbers. Factors are the numbers that "go into" your number evenly. Below we will list the factors of 56 and 64 respectively:

Factors of 56	Factors of 64
1, 56	1, 64
2, 28	2, 32
4, 14	4, 16
7, 8	8

Notice how we listed these factors in a methodical fashion. For example, $1 \times 56 = 56$, so we listed 1 and 56. $2 \times 28 = 56$, so we listed 2, 28. If you keep your scratch work orderly, it is easy to spot your answer. What is the largest *factor* that these two numbers have in common? 8.

77. **a.** The *quotient* is the solution to a division problem, and in this case the division problem is *"nine divided by three,"* or $9 \div 3$. The given statement says: *"The quotient of nine divided by three is decreased by one,"* so now we must decrease the quotient by 1. The answer is: $9 \div 3 - 1$.

78. **d.** First, multiply 250×213 to get 53,250. Next, because there is a 5 in the *tens place*, you round up in the *hundreds place* to get 53,300.

79. **d.** First, you should list all the factors of each of the given numbers. Remember that *factors* are the numbers that "go into" your number evenly.

Factors of 56	Factors of 96
1, 56,	1, 96
2, 28,	2, 48
4, 14,	3, 32
7, 8	4, 24,
	6, 16
	8, 12

The factors that they have in common are high-lighted in gray. None of the answer choices represent factors that these numbers have in common, so choose **d**, none of the above.

80. b. When adding a negative number, such as -6, to a positive number, such as 13, you subtract 6 from 13. $13 + (-6) = 13 - 6 = 7$. You can think about this in terms of money and debt: If you owed 6 dollars to someone and you had 13 dollars, the amount that is actually yours is $7.

81. c. When you square a negative number, or raise a negative number to any even power, the result is a positive number. So, $(-9)^2 = 81$.

82. d. When you raise a negative number to any odd power, the result is a negative number. So, $(-2)^5 = -2 \times -2 \times -2 \times -2 \times -2 = -32$.

83. c. $3 \times 3 \times 3 \times 3 \times 3$ is the same as 3^5. When you raise a number to a power, you are telling how many times you are multiplying the number by itself. $3^2 = 3 \times 3$, $3^3 = 3 \times 3 \times 3$, $3^4 = 3 \times 3 \times 3 \times 3$, and so forth. 3! is three *factorial*, and is written as $3 \times 2 \times 1$, so **a** is wrong. If you were to multiply out $3 \times 3 \times 3 \times 3 \times 3$, you would get 243, thus **d** is wrong as well.

84. c. $11^2 = 121$, so $\sqrt{121} = 11$.

85. b. 7 oz. is less than 9 oz., so 7 oz. < 9 oz., and choice **b** is correct. Remember, when you see the greater than and less than symbols, the symbol opens up to the larger number.

86. c. Twenty-three thousand, five hundred and seventeen can be written as the numeral 23,517. Below is a reminder of the names for all the places to the left of the decimal point:

ten thousands	thousands	hundreds	tens	units (ones)
2	3	5	1	7.

87. d. 13^3 can be rewritten as $13 \times 13 \times 13 = 169 \times 13 = 2{,}197$.

88. c. When multiplying two negative numbers (or any even amount of negative numbers), you will get a positive number. $(-8) \times (-5) = 40$.

89. a. Eleven thousand, two hundred and fifty-seven is expressed mathematically as 11,257. Below is a reminder of the names for all the places to the left of the decimal point:

ten thousands	thousands	hundreds	tens	units (ones)
1	1	2	5	7.

90. b. $4 \text{ cm} + 8 \text{ cm} \geq 7 \text{ cm} + 5 \text{ cm}$ is a true inequality. You can simplify both sides to get $12 \text{ cm} \geq 12 \text{ cm}$. This is true because the symbol in the middle means "*Greater than or equal to.*"

SET 4

91. b. If you look closely at the sequence 31 23 17 13 ___, you should first note that the numbers are decreasing. How much are they decreasing by? Well from 31 to 23 we decreased by 8. From 23 to 17 we decreased by 6. From 17 to 13 we decreased by 4. From 13 to the blank space we should decrease by 2. $13 - 2 = 11$.

92. d. Order matters when writing a ratio. This is because you are comparing one kind of a part to another kind of a part. For example if there was a 20 to 50 ratio of boys to girls, we could write this as 20:50. However, it would be wrong to write 50:20 because there are not 50 boys for every 20 girls. Therefore, **a** is wrong. If we take the correct ratio 20:50, we are allowed to divide both sides by 10 to get 2:5. Thus **d** is correct.

93. b. To find the median score, you first must list all of the scores in order: 3 7 8 10 12 13 14. The middle number will be your median: 3 7 8 **10** 12 13 14. Hence, 10 is the median. Note, that if there are ever two middle numbers (i.e., when taking the median of an even number of numbers), you simply take the average of the 2 middle numbers.

94. a. To equally divide the $540 bill among 6 housemates, you divide $540 by 6: $540 ÷ 6 = $90.

95. c. Because the term *mean* is another term for *average*, you know that **d** must be wrong. We will need to calculate the mean and the median. The formula for calculating the *mean* (average) is:

$$\text{Mean} = \frac{\text{sum of all values}}{\text{\# of values}}$$

Here the sum of all the values is 12 + 14 + 15 + 19 + 20 + 22 = 102, and the number of values is 6. Thus the average is $\frac{102}{6} = 17$.

To find the *median*, you arrange all of the numbers in order (luckily they are in order) and find the middle term: 12 14 **15 19** 20 22. Notice that there are 2 middle terms, so we need to find their average: (15 + 19) ÷ 2 = 34 ÷ 2 = 17. Thus, the mean = the median.

96. a. The mode of a set of numbers is the number that appears the most. Looking at the numbers: 35 52 17 23 51 52 18 32, we see that 52 appears twice.

35 **52** 17 23 51 **52** 18 32

Thus, the mode is 52. Note that choice **c** represents the median, and choice **b** represents the average of the given numbers.

97. c. Here you need to know the formula for calculating the average, which is also known as the mean:

$$\text{Average} = \frac{\text{sum of all values}}{\text{\# of values}}$$

Here we know that the average is 13 and that 5 CDs were purchased. We have $13 = \frac{(\text{sum of all values})}{5}$. Multiplying both sides by 5, we get 65 = sum of all CDs. We know that she bought 3 CDs at $12 each, a fourth for $15, and we need to figure out what the fifth CD cost. We will put a "?" in for the fifth CD.

$$65 = \text{sum of all CDs}$$
$$65 = 12 + 12 + 12 + 15 + ?$$
$$65 = 36 + 15 + ?$$
$$65 = 51 + ?$$
$$14 = ?$$

This means that the fifth CD cost $14.

98. c. Remember that ratios are used to represent part to part. Here we need to make a ratio for carbon dioxide to oxygen. Using the numbers given in the question, carbon dioxide to oxygen is 35: 20,945. Notice that there is a lot more oxygen than carbon dioxide. Choice **a** is wrong because this ratio (20,945: 35) specifies a lot more carbon dioxide than oxygen. Because our correct ratio 35: 20,945 isn't among the choices, we will reduce it by dividing it by 5. The new and equivalent ratio is 7: 4189, choice **c**.

99. **d.** Given the total cost is \$14,200, we can first subtract the \$1600 off due to the trade. \$14,200 − \$1600 = \$12,600. There is \$12,600 to be paid off throughout 5 years, or 60 months. (5 years × 12 months per year = 60 months.) Thus, his monthly payment will be \$12,600 ÷ 60 = \$210.

100. **b.** First, notice that the numbers in the sequence are increasing.

$$11\ 28\ \underline{\ \ \ }\ 62\ 79$$

To go from 11 to 28, it *increased by 17*. To go from 62 to 79, it *increased by 17*. Let's increase 28 by 17. 28 + 17 = 45. Does 45 make the sequence work? 45 + 17 = 62. Yes! This works:

$$11\ 28\ \mathbf{45}\ 62\ 79$$

The missing number is 45, choice **b**.

101. **b.** To figure out the probability for the given outcome, you need to calculate the total possible outcomes. We know that the record company brought 300 rap cassettes, 500 hard rock cassettes, 200 easy listening cassettes, and 400 country cassettes. The total possible outcomes equal 300 + 500 + 200 + 400 = 1400. The outcomes that fit the criteria in the question = 200. This is because 200 easy listening cassettes will be given out. This means that the chance of getting an easy listening cassette will be $\frac{200}{1400}$. This reduces to $\frac{1}{7}$.

102. **d.** To solve this question, we need to set up a proportion. The units must match on both sides of the proportion, so we will change 10 minutes into seconds by multiplying by 60 (there are 60 seconds in a minute). Thus, we need to know how many blinks will occur in 10 min × 60 $\frac{\text{sec}}{\text{min}}$ = 600 sec. Our proportion looks like this:

$$\frac{2\text{ blinks}}{3\text{ sec}} = \frac{?\text{ blinks}}{600\text{ sec}}$$

We cross-multiply to get: (600)(2) = (3)(?), or 1200 = (3)(?). Dividing both sides by 3, we get 400 = ?. The light will blink 400 times in 10 minutes.

103. **b.** To find $\sqrt{35}$, you need to find out what number, when squared, will yield 35. If you notice that $6^2 = 36$ and $5^2 = 25$, you know that the number you need must be between 5 and 6.

104. **c.** $4 × 10^4$ mm = 4 × 10,000 = 40,000 mm. $2 × 10^2$ mm = 2 × 100 = 200. How many times larger is 40,000 than 200? 40,000 ÷ 200 = 200. Thus, the first particle is 200 times larger than the second.

105. **a.** We will need to set up a proportion:

$$\frac{8\text{ people}}{2\text{ plants}} = \frac{?\text{ people}}{30\text{ plants}}$$

Next, we cross multiply: (8)(30) = (2)(?). Dividing both sides by 2, we get:

$$\frac{(8)(30)}{2} = ?$$

Thus, the number of people needed can be represented by $\frac{(8)(30)}{2}$, which is the same as choice **a**: 8 × 30 ÷ 2.

SET 5

106. **b.** If each car can carry 54 people, and there are 324 people, you just divide the number of people by the capacity of the car (54) to figure out how many cars are necessary. The correct calculation is 324 ÷ 54.

107. **b.** You know that the concentration of carbon monoxide did not remain constant, so **d** must be wrong. Let's see which answer choice makes sense. We'll make a chart for all of the possibilities:

Concentration of Carbon Monoxide			
Time	If Quadrupled Every Hour	If Tripled Every Hour	If Doubled Every Hour
9 A.M.	50 ppm	50 ppm	50 ppm
10 A.M.	200 ppm	150 ppm	100 ppm
11 A.M.	800 ppm	450 ppm	200 ppm
12 noon	3200 ppm	1350 ppm	400 ppm
	Too high! Choice **a** is wrong.	Exactly right! Pick choice **b**.	Too low! Choice **c** is wrong.

108. **c.** Because this question requires an answer in dollars, we will first convert the 95 cents into dollars. 95 cents = $.95. If 1 gallon costs $.95, we simply multiply this price by 3 to get the price of 3 gallons: $3 \times .95 = \$2.85$.

109. **a.** First, calculate the number of possible outcomes. The possibilities are: 1, 2, 3, 4, 5, or 6. Thus, there are 6 possible outcomes. Next, underline the outcomes that satisfy the condition given in the question. Which of these numbers are multiples of 3? 1, 2, **3**, 4, 5, **6**. Notice that only 2 outcomes out of a total of 6 outcomes are multiples of 3. Thus, the answer would be $\frac{2}{6}$ which reduces to $\frac{1}{3}$.

110. **d.** To answer this question we will use *conversion factors*. Don't be intimidated by the term; a *conversion factor* is a special way of multiplying by one. To convert the miles into feet, we will multiply by the conversion factor $\frac{5280\,\text{feet}}{1\,\text{mile}}$. We will also need a conversion factor to change the feet into inches, so we will also multiply by $\frac{12\,\text{inches}}{1\,\text{foot}}$. Thus, 5 miles = $5\text{ miles} \times \frac{5280\,\text{ft.}}{\text{mile}} \times \frac{12\,\text{inches}}{1\,\text{ft.}} = $ 316,800 inches.

111. **d.** We know that Darren's band played for 1 hour and 35 minutes, and Ray's band played for 1 hour and 40 minutes.

112. **c.** 12 ounces + 8 ounces = 20 ounces. Because 20 ounces isn't a choice, we know that we need to rename some of these ounces as pounds. 1 lb. = 16 oz., so 20 ounces can be thought of as 16 oz. + 4 oz. = 1 lb. + 4 oz.

113. **a.** From 8:35 A.M. until 12:35 P.M. would be 4 hours. To get from 12:35 P.M. to 1 P.M. would be how many more minutes?

It would be another 25 minutes to reach 1:00. Then we need another 13 minutes to reach 1:13 P.M. So, the total amount of time would be 4 hrs. + 25 min. + 13 min. = 4 hrs. 38 min.

114. **b.** Just stack similar units and add:

2 hr. 15 min.
+ 4 hr. 10 min.
6 hr. 25 min.

115. **d.** You simply put 35 in for C in the given equation: $F = \frac{9}{5}C + 32$; so $F = \frac{9}{5}(35) + 32$. Notice that you can cross the 5 out of the denominator and reduce the 35 to 7:

$$F = \frac{9}{5}(\overset{7}{\cancel{35}}) + 32 = 9 \cdot 7 + 32 = 63 + 32 = 95°\text{ F.}$$

116. **b.** First stack similar units and add:

2 ft. 5 in.
2 yd. 1 ft. 3 in.
4 yd.   8 in.
+   3 ft. 2 in.
6 yd. 6 ft. 18 in.

Because we know that 12 in. = 1 foot, we can rewrite 18 in. as 18 in. = 12 in. + 6 in. = 1 ft. + 6 in.

```
  6 yd.   6 ft.   18 in.
+         1 ft.    6 in.
  6 yd.   7 ft.    6 in.
```

117. **d.** First, set up your subtraction problem:

```
    3'   3"
  − 1'  10"
```

Because we cannot subtract 10″ from 3″, we will rename one of the given 3′ as 12 inches:

```
    2'  15"
    3'   3"
  − 1'  10"
    1'   5"
```

118. **c.** 8 pints are poured out. We can convert this amount into quarts by multiplying by the conversion factor $\frac{1\,\text{quart}}{2\,\text{pints}}$. Thus, we get 8 pints $\times \frac{1\,\text{qt.}}{2\,\text{pints}}$ = 4 quarts were poured out. We can set up a subtraction equation as follows:

```
  1 gal.  2 qt.
  −        4 qt.
```

Because we cannot subtract 4 qt. from 2 qt., we will need to rename the gallon as 4 quarts.

```
          6 qt
  1 gal.  2 qt.
  −        4 qt.
          2 qt.
```

Thus, 2 quarts of punch remain in the container.

119. **b.**

```
    3'    7"
  + 5'    8"
    8'   15"
```

Because 12″ = 1 ft., we can rename 15″ as 15″ = 12″ + 3″ = 1 ft. + 3″. Thus, the answer is 8′ + 1′ + 3″ = 9′ 3″.

120. **a.** Let's convert all of the answer choices into cups to see which represents the largest volume of liquid:

Choice **a**: 7 quarts $\times \frac{2\,\text{pints}}{1\,\text{qt.}} \times \frac{2\,\text{cups}}{1\,\text{pint}}$ = 28 cups

Choice **b**: 5 pints $\times \frac{2\,\text{cups}}{1\,\text{pint}}$ = 10 cups

Choice **c**: 3 cups

Choice **d**: 1 gallon $\times \frac{4\,\text{qt.}}{1\,\text{gal.}} \times \frac{2\,\text{pints}}{1\,\text{qt.}} \times \frac{2\,\text{cups}}{1\,\text{pint}}$ = 16 cups

Thus, **a** represents the largest volume.

SET 6

121. **d.** The weight in pounds per cubic feet of wet sand is 120. The weight for pumice is 40. The ratio is then 120:40. This reduces to 3:1.

122. **b.** First, let's add up all of the donations listed in the chart: $525 + $440 + $615 = $1580. Whatever Jen gave plus the $1580 will yield $2055. We can just subtract $1580 from $2055 to get Jen's donation: $2055 − $1580 = $475.

123. **a.** The formula for calculating the mean (average) is:

$$\text{Mean} = \frac{\text{sum of all values}}{\text{\# of values}}$$

The sum of all the values given is: 75 + 81 + 93 + 77 + 84 = 410. The number of values (scores) is 5. Thus, the mean = $\frac{410}{5}$ = 82.

124. **b.** First, note that this is a plot of *millions of dollars* versus *quarters*. Next, use the code to the right of the diagram to see that the white bars represent the "West" revenues. Looking at the white bar for each of the first *three* quarters, we know that the amount of revenue is: 40 million + 45 million + 50 million = 135 million.

125. a. For the third quarter, the black bar, which represents the revenues for East, goes up to 40 million dollars. For the first quarter, the gray bar, which represents the revenues for North, goes up to 20 million dollars. Thus, the East made 40 million − 20 million = 20 million dollars more than the North for the time periods cited.

126. b. Fill in the missing line, based on your judgment:

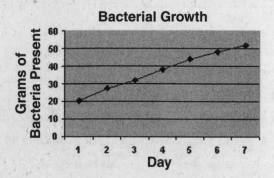

38 is the best approximation. The other answers would be too far above or below the line drawn.

127. c. First, look at the black bar for the year 1997. This bar represents the cost, in dollars, of gas in 1997, which is $600. Next, we will look at the white bar for the year 1998. This bar represents the cost, in dollars, for oil. This bar goes up to $500. Next, we subtract: $600 − $500 = $100.

128. d. The online purchase profits are represented by a light gray bar. Looking from each year to the next, we see that the size of this bar doubles. Thus, **b** is true. Charge card interest is represented by a black bar. This bar also doubles for each year shown. Thus, **c** is also true. The answer is then **d**: "both b and c are true."

129. c. Let's go through the choices:
   a. management + graphics = 375 + 300 = 675 *Nope!*
   b. graphics + marketing = 300 + 450 = 750 *Nope!*
   c. management + sales = 375 + 270 = 645 *Yes!*

Choice **c** is correct.

130. b. The black piece of the pie represents 300 programming students. The dark gray piece of the pie represents 600 multimedia students. Thus, the ratio of programming students to multimedia students is 300:600. This reduces to 1:2.

SECTION 2—FRACTIONS

SET 7

131. b. Because one of 3 pieces is shaded, we know that $\frac{1}{3}$ (*one third*) of the figure is shaded.

132. d. Because 3 out of 4 pieces are shaded, we know that $\frac{3}{4}$ (*three quarters*) of the figure is shaded.

133. d. Because 3 out of 8 pieces are shaded, we know that $\frac{3}{8}$ (*three eighths*) of the figure is shaded.

134. c. Because 6 out of 16 pieces are shaded, we know that $\frac{6}{16}$ (*six sixteenths*) of the figure is shaded. By dividing the numerator (top) and denominator (bottom) by 2, we can reduce $\frac{6}{16}$ to $\frac{3}{8}$.

135. a. Because 2 out of 4 pieces are shaded, we know that $\frac{2}{4}$ (*two fourths*) of the figure is shaded. By dividing the numerator (top) and denominator (bottom) by 2, we can reduce $\frac{2}{4}$ to $\frac{1}{2}$.

136. b. To change the improper fraction $\frac{132}{12}$ to a whole number, simply divide 132 by 12: $132 \div 12 = 11$.

137. c. The term *"improper fraction"* is used to describe a fraction whose top part (numerator) is larger than its bottom part (denominator). To convert $3\frac{2}{3}$ to an improper fraction we multiply 3×3, add 2, and then stick it all over 3:

$$3 \overset{times}{\underset{}{\,}} \frac{2}{3}\big)\, plus$$

So, we get $\frac{11}{3}$.

138. c. To change the improper fraction $\frac{12}{4}$ to a whole number, simply divide 12 by 4: $12 \div 4 = 3$.

139. a. Multiply the whole number, 1, by the denominator and add the numerator. Then stick this value over 7:

$$1 \overset{times}{\underset{}{\,}} \frac{5}{7}\big)\, plus$$

Thus, we get $\frac{12}{7}$.

140. d. First, we convert $2\frac{1}{3}$ to an improper fraction by multiplying the whole number, 2, by the denominator and adding the numerator. We will stick this value over 3.

$$2 \overset{times}{\underset{}{\,}} \frac{1}{3}\big)\, plus$$

Thus, $\frac{2}{3} = \frac{7}{3}$. To take the reciprocal of $\frac{7}{3}$, we just switch the numerator with the denominator. This yields $\frac{3}{7}$.

141. b. The term *"improper fraction"* is used to describe a fraction whose top part (numerator) is larger than its bottom part (denominator). Only choice **b** fits this description.

142. c. The easiest way to compare the values of these fractions is to convert them into decimals by dividing their *tops* by their *bottoms*.

	Fraction	Decimal
a.	$\frac{5}{8}$	.625
b.	$\frac{2}{3}$	.6666 repeating
c.	$\frac{8}{11}$	.727272 repeating
d.	$\frac{4}{10}$	.4

Thus, choice **c** is the greatest.

143. a. $\frac{1}{4} = .25$ and $\frac{2}{3} = .6666$ repeating, so we need to see which fraction has a decimal equivalent within this range.

	Fraction	Decimal
a.	$\frac{5}{8}$	.625
b.	$\frac{5}{6}$	.8333 repeating
c.	$\frac{8}{11}$	.727272 repeating
d.	$\frac{7}{10}$	.7

Thus, choice **a** is between $\frac{1}{4}$ and $\frac{2}{3}$.

144. b. Just divide 17 by 3. You get 5 with a remainder of 2. Since we are talking about thirds (the original denominator was 3), stick the remainder over 3. Thus, the answer is $5\frac{2}{3}$.

145. c. Divide the numerator by the denominator and stick the remainder over the denominator. In other words, $15 \div 2 = 7$, remainder 1. We put the remainder over 2, so the complete answer is $7\frac{1}{2}$.

SET 8

146. d. $\frac{1}{9} + \frac{5}{9} = \frac{6}{9}$. Dividing top and bottom by 3, this reduces to $\frac{2}{3}$.

147. c. $\frac{5}{8} - \frac{3}{8} = \frac{2}{8}$. Dividing top and bottom by 2, this reduces to $\frac{1}{4}$.

148. a. First we'll find the LCD (least common denominator). In this case, it is $9 \times 4 = 36$. Converting, we get $\left(\frac{5}{9}\right)\left(\frac{4}{4}\right) - \left(\frac{1}{4}\right)\left(\frac{9}{9}\right) = \frac{20}{36} - \frac{9}{36} = \frac{11}{36}$.

149. b. Let's look at this problem step by step:

Original Question: $9\frac{5}{6} - 7\frac{1}{8}$

1. Convert to improper fractions:

$9^{times\,\frac{5}{6}}plus$ $\qquad$ $7^{times\,\frac{1}{8}}plus$

$= \frac{59}{6}$ $\qquad$ $= \frac{57}{8}$

$\frac{59}{6}$ $\quad - \quad$ $\frac{57}{8}$

2. Find LCD: $\frac{59}{6} \cdot \frac{4}{4}$ $\qquad$ $\frac{57}{8} \cdot \frac{3}{3}$

$\frac{236}{24}$ $\quad - \quad$ $\frac{171}{24}$

3. Solve: $\frac{65}{24}$

4. Convert to a mixed number: $2\frac{17}{24}$

150. b. $-\frac{3}{7} - \frac{4}{7} = -\frac{7}{7} = -1$.

151. d. Let's find the LCD (*least common denominator*) for these fractions. In this case, we get $5 \times 7 = 35$, as the LCD. Converting, we get: $\left(-\frac{2}{5}\right)\left(\frac{7}{7}\right) - \left(\frac{3}{7}\right)\left(\frac{5}{5}\right) = -\frac{14}{35} - \frac{15}{35} = -\frac{29}{35}$.

152. c. First change $1\frac{2}{7}$ into an improper fraction. We multiply 1×7 plus 2 and stick this value over 7:

$1^{times\,\frac{2}{7}}plus$

Thus $1\frac{2}{7} = \frac{9}{7}$. Our expression is now $\frac{9}{7} + \frac{1}{9}$. We need to find the least common denominator (LCD). In this case 9×7, or 63, is the LCD. Converting, we get: $\left(\frac{9}{7}\right)\left(\frac{9}{9}\right) + \left(\frac{1}{9}\right)\left(\frac{7}{7}\right) = \frac{81}{63} + \frac{7}{63} = \frac{88}{63}$. Divide 88 by 63 to get the mixed number $1\frac{25}{63}$.

153. c. Let's look at the question step by step:

Original Question: $2\frac{5}{8} + 3\frac{1}{4} - 5\frac{5}{6}$

1. Convert to improper fractions:

$2^{times\,\frac{5}{8})\,plus}$ $3^{times\,\frac{1}{4})\,plus}$ $5^{times\,\frac{5}{6})\,plus}$

$= \frac{21}{8}$ $= \frac{13}{4}$ $= \frac{35}{6}$

$\frac{21}{8}$ $+$ $\frac{13}{4}$ $-$ $\frac{35}{6}$

2. Find LCD: $\frac{21}{8} \cdot \frac{3}{3}$ $\frac{13}{4} \cdot \frac{6}{6}$ $\frac{35}{6} \cdot \frac{4}{4}$

$\frac{63}{24}$ $+$ $\frac{78}{24}$ $-$ $\frac{140}{24}$

3. Solve: $\frac{141}{24} - \frac{140}{24} =$

$\frac{1}{24}$

154. a. Just multiply numerator × numerator and denominator × denominator: $\frac{5}{8} \times \frac{4}{7} = \frac{20}{56}$. Reducing, we get $\frac{5}{14}$. Alternatively, when examining $\frac{5}{8} \times \frac{4}{7}$, note that you can cross out the 4 and change the 8 to a 2:

$\frac{5}{\underset{2}{8}} \times \frac{4}{7} = \frac{5}{14}$

155. d. First we will convert these mixed numbers into improper fractions: $2\frac{2}{3} = 2$ times 3 plus 2, all over 3:

$2^{times\,\frac{2}{3})\,plus}$

$= \frac{8}{3}$.

Converting $8\frac{1}{5}$ we get: 8 times 5 plus 1, all over 5:

$8^{times\,\frac{1}{5})\,plus}$

$= \frac{41}{5}$. The question is now: $\frac{8}{3} \times \frac{41}{5} = \frac{328}{15}$. Dividing top by bottom, we get 21, remainder 13. We put the remainder over 15 to yield $21\frac{13}{15}$.

156. b. First we will convert these mixed numbers into improper fractions: $2\frac{3}{5} = 2$ times 5 plus 3, all over 5:

$2^{times\,\frac{3}{5})\,plus}$

$= \frac{13}{5}$.

Converting $1\frac{2}{3}$ we get: 1 times 3 plus 2, all over 3:

$1^{times\,\frac{2}{3})\,plus}$

$= \frac{5}{3}$. The question is now: $\frac{13}{5} \times \frac{5}{3}$. Notice that the fives cancel:

$\frac{13}{5} \times \frac{5}{3} = \frac{13}{3}$

We convert $\frac{13}{3}$ into a mixed number by dividing: $13 \div 3 = 4$, remainder 1. We put the remainder over 3 to yield $4\frac{1}{3}$.

157. c. First, we convert the mixed numbers into improper fractions: $-2\frac{5}{7} = -2$ times 7 plus 5, all over 7:

$-2^{times\,\frac{5}{7})\,plus}$

$= -\frac{19}{7}$.

Converting $4\frac{1}{5}$ we get: 4 times 5 plus 1, all over 5:

$4^{times\,\frac{1}{5})\,plus}$

$= \frac{21}{5}$. The question is now: $-\frac{19}{7} \times \frac{21}{5}$. Notice that we can cross out the 7 and change the 21 to 3:

$-\frac{19}{7} \times \frac{\overset{3}{21}}{5} = -\frac{57}{5}$

We convert $-\frac{57}{5}$ into a mixed number by dividing: $-57 \div 5 = 11$, remainder 2. We put the remainder over 5 to yield $-11\frac{2}{5}$.

158. d. This question is really just another "multiplication with fractions" problem. Substituting the sides into the formula *Area = length × width*, we get $Area = 20\frac{1}{3} \times 10\frac{1}{2}$. First, we'll convert the mixed numbers into improper fractions: $20\frac{1}{3} = 20$ times 3 plus 1, all over 3:

$$20 \overset{times}{\frown} \frac{1}{3} \big) plus$$

$$= \frac{61}{3}.$$

Converting $10\frac{1}{2}$ we get: 10 times 2 plus 1, all over 2:

$$10 \overset{times}{\frown} \frac{1}{2} \big) plus$$

$= \frac{21}{5}$. The question is now: $\frac{61}{3} \times \frac{21}{2}$. Notice that we can cross out the 3 and change the 21 to 7:

$$\frac{61}{\cancel{3}} \times \frac{\overset{7}{\cancel{21}}}{2} = \frac{427}{2}$$

We convert $\frac{427}{2}$ into a mixed number by dividing: $427 \div 2 = 213$, remainder 1. We put the remainder over 2 to yield $213\frac{1}{2}$.

159. d. We are looking for the *reciprocal* of $\frac{21}{42}$. When we take the reciprocal, we just switch the top and bottom:

$$\frac{21}{42} \;\text{—}reciprocal\text{➔}\; \frac{42}{21}.$$

This is answer choice **d**, so we need not reduce.

160. a. When dividing fractions, we actually change the problem into a multiplication problem. We change $5 \div \frac{2}{7}$ into a multiplication problem by taking the *reciprocal* of $\frac{2}{7}$. To take the reciprocal, we just switch the top and bottom:

$$\frac{2}{7} \;\text{—}reciprocal\text{➔}\; \frac{7}{2}.$$

Now the original problem, $5 \div \frac{2}{7}$, can be written as $5 \times \frac{7}{2}$, which equals $\frac{35}{2}$. We convert $\frac{35}{2}$ into a mixed number by dividing: $35 \div 2 = 17$, re-

mainder 1. We put the remainder over 2 to yield $17\frac{1}{2}$.

161. c. We change the division problem $\frac{18}{5} \div \frac{9}{20}$ into a multiplication problem by taking the *reciprocal* of $\frac{9}{20}$. When we take the reciprocal, we just switch the top and bottom:

$$\frac{9}{20} \;\text{—}reciprocal\text{➔}\; \frac{20}{9}.$$

Thus, $\frac{18}{5} \div \frac{9}{20} = \frac{18}{5} \times \frac{20}{9}$. Next, we cancel out:

$$\frac{\overset{2}{\cancel{18}}}{5} \times \frac{\overset{4}{\cancel{20}}}{\cancel{9}} = 8$$

162. b. First, let's convert $1\frac{2}{7}$ into an improper fraction: We multiply 1×7, add 2, and then put this value over 7:

$$1 \overset{times}{\frown} \frac{2}{7} \big) plus$$

$$= \frac{9}{7}$$

Now, our question is $\frac{9}{7} \div \frac{9}{11}$. Because dividing by $\frac{9}{11}$ is the same as multiplying by $\frac{11}{9}$ (the *reciprocal* of $\frac{9}{11}$), we know $\frac{9}{7} \div \frac{9}{11} = \frac{9}{7} \times \frac{11}{9}$. Note that the nines cancel:

$$\frac{9}{7} \times \frac{11}{9} = \frac{11}{7} = 11 \div 7 = 1, \text{ remainder } 4.$$

We put the remainder over 7 to yield $1\frac{4}{7}$.

163. c. First, let's convert $1\frac{3}{8}$ into an improper fraction: We multiply 1×8, add 3, and then put this value over 8:

$$1 \overset{times}{\frown} \frac{3}{8} \big) plus$$

$$= \frac{11}{8}$$

Now, we'll convert $1\frac{1}{4}$ to an improper fraction. We multiply 1×4, add 1, and then put this value over 4:

$$1 \overset{times}{\frown} \frac{1}{4} \big) plus$$

$$= \frac{5}{4}$$

Now, our question is $\frac{11}{8} \div \frac{5}{4}$. Because dividing by $\frac{5}{4}$ is the same as multiplying by $\frac{4}{5}$ (the *reciprocal* of $\frac{5}{4}$), we know $\frac{11}{8} \div \frac{5}{4} = \frac{11}{8} \times \frac{4}{5}$. Notice that we can cross out a 4 and change the 8 to a 2:

$$\frac{11}{\underset{2}{8}} \times \frac{4}{5} = \frac{11}{10} = 11 \div 10 = 1, \text{ remainder } 1.$$

We put the remainder over 10 to yield $1\frac{1}{10}$.

164. d. $6 \div \frac{12}{13} = 6 \times \frac{13}{12} =$

$\underset{2}{\cancel{6}} \times \frac{13}{\cancel{12}} = \frac{13}{2} = 13 \div 2 = 6, \text{ remainder } 1.$

We put the remainder over 2 to yield $6\frac{1}{2}$.

165. b. First, let's convert $3\frac{1}{3}$ into an improper fraction: We multiply 3×3, add 1, and then put this value over 3:

$$3\!\overset{times}{\underset{}{}}\!\left(\frac{1}{3}\right)\text{plus}$$

$$= \frac{10}{3}$$

Now, our question is $\frac{10}{3} \div \frac{5}{9}$. Because dividing by $\frac{5}{9}$ is the same as multiplying by $\frac{9}{5}$ (the *reciprocal* of $\frac{5}{9}$), we know $\frac{10}{3} \div \frac{5}{9} = \frac{10}{3} \times \frac{9}{5}$. Note that we can do some canceling:

$$\frac{\overset{2}{\cancel{10}}}{3} \times \frac{\overset{3}{\cancel{9}}}{\cancel{5}} = 6$$

SET 9

166. d. Looking at the chart, we read the values for Tuesday and Thursday:

Laurie's Jogging Log

Day	Miles Jogged
Sunday	4
Monday	3
Tuesday	$3\frac{1}{3}$
Wednesday	5
Thursday	$2\frac{1}{3}$
Friday	$2\frac{2}{3}$
Saturday	3

When we compute a *difference*, we subtract: $3\frac{1}{3} - 2\frac{1}{3}$. Thus, **d** is correct.

167. b. First, we use the chart to find out how many miles she jogged on Thursday and Friday.

Laurie's Jogging Log

Day	Miles Jogged
Sunday	4
Monday	3
Tuesday	$3\frac{1}{3}$
Wednesday	5
Thursday	$2\frac{1}{3}$
Friday	$2\frac{2}{3}$
Saturday	3

To *combine* these values, we add: $2\frac{1}{3} + 2\frac{2}{3}$. Because we are dealing with thirds, we can add the $\frac{1}{3}$ to the $\frac{2}{3}$ to get $\frac{3}{3}$, or 1. So $2\frac{1}{3} + 2\frac{2}{3} = 2 + 2 + 1 = 5$ miles.

168. c. The formula for average is:

$$\text{Average} = \frac{\text{sum of all values}}{\text{\# of values}}$$

First, let's add up all of the *nice*, whole numbers:

Laurie's Jogging Log

Day	Miles Jogged
Sunday	4
Monday	3
Tuesday	$3\frac{1}{3}$
Wednesday	5
Thursday	$2\frac{1}{3}$
Friday	$2\frac{2}{3}$
Saturday	3

$4 + 3 + 5 + 3 = 15$ miles

Now, we add in $3\frac{1}{3}$, $2\frac{1}{3}$, and $2\frac{2}{3}$. Note that in **Question 167**, we calculated that $2\frac{1}{3} + 2\frac{2}{3} = 5$ miles. So, the sum of all values would be: $15 + 5 + 3\frac{1}{3} = 23\frac{1}{3}$ miles. Because there are 7 values, we can substitute into our average formula:

$$\text{Average} = \frac{\text{sum of all values}}{\text{\# of values}} = \frac{23\frac{1}{3}}{7}$$

Now we have a fraction *division* problem: $23\frac{1}{3} \div 7$. Let's convert $23\frac{1}{3}$ into an improper fraction. We multiply 23×3, add 1, and then put this value over 3:

$23\overset{times}{\longrightarrow} \tfrac{1}{3})\,plus$

$= \frac{70}{3}$

The expression is now: $\frac{70}{3} \div 7$. This is the same as $\frac{70}{3} \div \frac{7}{1}$. Because dividing by $\frac{7}{1}$ is the same as multiplying by $\frac{1}{7}$ (the *reciprocal* of $\frac{7}{1}$), we know $\frac{70}{3} \div \frac{7}{1} = \frac{70}{3} \times \frac{1}{7}$. Note that we can cross out a 7 and change the 70 to a 10:

$\frac{\cancel{70}^{10}}{3} \times \frac{1}{\cancel{7}} = \frac{10}{3} = 10 \div 3 = 3$, remainder 1.

We put the remainder over 3 to yield $3\frac{1}{3}$.

169. c. The term "*improper fraction*" is used to describe a fraction whose top part (numerator) is larger than its bottom part (denominator). Only choice **c** fits this description.

170. d. Dividing by $\frac{3}{5}$ is the same as multiplying by the reciprocal of $\frac{3}{5}$, which is $\frac{5}{3}$. Thus, **d** is correct. Remember that when finding the reciprocal, you just switch the top and bottom:

$$\frac{3}{5} \xrightarrow{reciprocal} \frac{5}{3}$$

171. a. Sebastian will pay $\frac{2}{3}$ of \$360,000, in cash. Mathematically, "*of*" means multiply, so Sebastian will pay $\frac{2}{3} \times \$360,000 =$

$\frac{2}{3} \times \$3\overset{120,000}{\cancel{60,000}} = \$240,000$

Rachel will pay $\frac{1}{4}$ of \$360,000 $= \frac{1}{4} \times \$360,000 =$

$\frac{1}{4} \times \$3\overset{90,000}{\cancel{60,000}} = \$90,000$

The amount needed would then be \$360,000 − \$240,000 − \$90,000 = \$30,000.

172. d. In a question like this, it is important not to be thrown by the information, and focus on what the question is really asking. The question really wants the sum of $+\frac{2}{3}$, $-\frac{1}{3}$, and $+\frac{1}{3}$, which would be $\frac{2}{3} + (-\frac{1}{3}) + \frac{1}{3}$. Notice that the $+\frac{1}{3}$ and $-\frac{1}{3}$ cancel each other out. The answer is $\frac{2}{3}$.

173. a. Because we need an answer in hours, let's convert the 45 minutes into hours. Because 1 hour = 60 minutes, we use the conversion factor $\frac{1 \text{ hr.}}{60 \text{ min.}}$. Thus, 45 min. $\times \frac{1 \text{ hr.}}{60 \text{ min.}} = \frac{45}{60}$ hr. $= \frac{3}{4}$ hr. If Greg completed $\frac{3}{4}$ of the job in $\frac{3}{4}$ of an hour, it is easy to see that he will complete $\frac{4}{4}$ of the job (the whole job) in $\frac{4}{4}$ of an hour (a whole hour). Thus, the answer is 1 hour.

174. d. Here we will use the conversion factor $\frac{144 \text{ bolts}}{1 \text{ gross}}$. We multiply: $3\frac{1}{2}$ gross $\times \frac{144 \text{ bolts}}{1 \text{ gross}} = \frac{7}{2}$ gross $\times \frac{144 \text{ bolts}}{1 \text{ gross}} = 7 \times \frac{72 \text{ bolts}}{1 \text{ gross}} = 504$ bolts.

175. d. Jaclyn is 16, and we know that Jane is $\frac{1}{2}$ as old as Jaclyn, so she must be 8. Jane is also $\frac{1}{3}$ as old as Zoey, so Zoey must be $8 \times 3 = 24$.

SET 10

176. b. 5 hours is $\frac{5}{8}$ of the 8 hours used in the chart to calculate the data, so take $\frac{5}{8}$ of the price: $\frac{5}{8} \cdot 120 = 5 \cdot 15 = \$75$.

177. b. According to the chart, the cost per year to run a dryer is \$120. If the cost per kwh was raised by $\frac{1}{4}$ in New York, this \$120 would increase by $\$120 \times \frac{1}{4} = \$30$. Thus, the cost to run a dryer each year in New York would be \$120 + \$30 = \$150. Similarly, if the cost per kwh was raised by $\frac{1}{8}$ in Florida, the \$120 currently listed in the chart would increase by $\$120 \times \frac{1}{8} = \$15$. Thus, the cost to run a dryer each year in Florida would be $120 + $15 = $135. In comparing the annual (yearly) cost for the energy used to run a dryer, the average New Yorker would have to pay $150 − $135 = $15 more.

178. **c.** We will set up a proportion:

$$\frac{\frac{1}{2}}{8\frac{1}{2}} = \frac{\frac{5}{8}}{?}$$

We cross multiply to get: $\frac{1}{2}(?) = (\frac{5}{8})(8\frac{1}{2})$, which means $\frac{1}{2}(?) = (\frac{5}{8})(\frac{17}{2})$, or $(\frac{1}{2})(?) = \frac{85}{16}$. Thus, $? = \frac{85}{16} \div \frac{1}{2} = \frac{85}{16} \times \frac{2}{1} = \frac{85}{8} = 10\frac{5}{8}$.

179. **c.** Notice that the numerators (tops) of each fraction remain the same. The denominators, however, are doubling. Therefore, the fraction that is missing is $\frac{1}{64}$.

180. **c.** If he starts with 200 gallons and ends with 17 gallons, we know that he will consume 200 − 17 = 183 gallons. He uses $7\frac{5}{8}$, or $\frac{61}{8}$ gallons per day. We know that $\frac{61}{8}$ gal per day *times* the number of days would *equal* 183 gallons. Mathematically, we express this statement as: $\frac{61}{8} \cdot ? = 183$. We divide both sides by $\frac{61}{8}$ to get: $? = 183 \div \frac{61}{8} = 183 \times \frac{8}{61} = \frac{1464}{61} = 24$ days.

181. **c.** Cathy earns $60,000. Darlene earns $\frac{1}{3}$ more than Cathy, which would be $\frac{1}{3} \times \$60,000 = \$20,000$ more. Thus, Darlene makes $60,000 + $20,000 = $80,000. Denise's stock portfolio is worth $\frac{1}{5}$ of Darlene's earnings, or $\frac{1}{5} \cdot \$80,000 = \$16,000$.

182. **d.** The $12,240 that Margaret received represents $\frac{3}{7}$ of the profit. Mathematically, "of" means *multiply*, so $\$12,240 = \frac{3}{7} \cdot$ profit. We divide both sides by $\frac{3}{7}$ to yield: $\$12,240 \div \frac{3}{7} =$ profit. This is the same as $\$12,240 \times \frac{7}{3} =$ profit, or $4,080 \times 7 =$ profit, so $28,560 =$ profit.

183. **b.** Just remember that when taking a fraction of some number, you are actually **multiplying** that number by the fraction. Let's look at what happens hour by hour.

Time	# Candies
Start	504
8–9 o'clock	minus $\frac{1}{8} \cdot 504$, or −63 = 441
9–10 o'clock	minus $\frac{2}{9} \cdot 441$, or −98 = 343
10–11 o'clock	minus $\frac{1}{7} \cdot 343$, or −49 = 294

Thus, there are 294 remaining.

184. **c.** Brian works $\frac{2}{5}$ of his usual 30 hours. "Of" means *multiply*, so he works $\frac{2}{5} \cdot 30 = 12$ hours. He makes $14 an hour, so we multiply: 12 hours × $14/hr. = $168.

185. **a.** First convert: $5\frac{1}{3}$ miles $= \frac{16}{3}$ miles. Now we will set up a proportion:

$$\frac{\frac{16}{3} \text{ mi.}}{1 \text{ hr.}} = \frac{16 \text{ mi.}}{? \text{hr.}}$$

We cross multiply to get: $\frac{16}{3} \cdot ? = 16$. We divide both sides by $\frac{16}{3}$ to yield: $? = 16 \div \frac{16}{3} = 16 \times \frac{3}{16} = 3$. Thus, he has been jogging for 3 hours.

186. **b.** After Monday, $\frac{1}{4}$ of the money is gone, so $\frac{3}{4}$ remains. Then, on Tuesday, Cassidy spent $\frac{1}{3}$ of that $\frac{3}{4}$, or $\frac{1}{3} \cdot \frac{3}{4} = \frac{1}{4}$. If she started Tuesday off with $\frac{3}{4}$ of her money and spends $\frac{1}{4}$, she has $\frac{3}{4} - \frac{1}{4} = \frac{2}{4}$ or $\frac{1}{2}$ her money left.

187. **c.** Normal speech is 50 dB, and it would take 150 dB to sustain hearing loss. The question basically asks what fraction times 150 would be 50? Mathematically, we can write: $? \cdot 150 = 50$. Dividing both sides by 150 yields: $? = \frac{50}{150} = \frac{1}{3}$.

SET 11

188. **b.** Because there was already $\frac{1}{5}$ of the capacity present, the added 20 L represents $\frac{4}{5}$ of the total capacity. We can ask: "20 liters is $\frac{4}{5}$ of what number?" We express this question mathematically by writing: $20 = \frac{4}{5} \cdot ?$ (Note that "is" is mathematically equivalent to "=," and "of" is mathematically equal to *times*.) We divide both sides of the equation by $\frac{4}{5}$ to get: $20 \div \frac{4}{5} = ?$, which is the same as $20 \times \frac{5}{4} = ?$, or $5 \times 5 = 25$.

189. **d.** Here we will set up a proportion:

$$\frac{\frac{1}{2}\text{ in.}}{1\text{ foot}} = \frac{4\frac{1}{2}\text{ in.}}{height\text{ in feet}}$$

This is represented by choice **d**. Notice that you need to have corresponding units in the numerators and corresponding units in the denominators of the proportion. For example, we have inches in the numerator on both sides of the equal sign.

190. **d.** If she completed $\frac{3}{4}$ of the job, then she still has $\frac{1}{4}$ of the job to do. We take $\frac{1}{4}$ of 64 to find out how many flyers she has left to hang: $\frac{1}{4} \cdot 64 = 16$ flyers.

191. **a.** Heather is cooking for 6 times as many people as the recipe was designed for ($24 \div 4 = 6$). Thus, she will need to add 6 times as much coriander as the recipe lists: $6 \cdot \frac{1}{2}$ tsp. $= 3$ tsp.

192. **a.** Now Heather is cooking for $26 \div 4 = 6\frac{1}{2}$ times as many people as the recipe provides for. Thus, she will need to add $6\frac{1}{2}$ times as much coriander as the recipe lists: $6\frac{1}{2} \cdot \frac{1}{2}$ tsp. $= \frac{13}{2} \cdot \frac{1}{2}$ tsp $= \frac{13}{4}$ tsp. $= 3\frac{1}{4}$ tsp.

193. **b.** We need to subtract: $12 - 3\frac{1}{8} = 11\frac{8}{8} - 3\frac{1}{8}$ $= 8\frac{7}{8}$ hours.

194. **c.** Just remember that when taking a fraction *of* some number, you are actually *multiplying* that number by the fraction. Let's look at what happens day by day:

Day	# Questions
Start	110
Friday	minus $\frac{1}{5} \cdot 110$, or $-22 = 88$
Saturday	minus $\frac{1}{4} \cdot 88$, or $-22 = 66$
10-11 o'clock	minus $\frac{1}{3} \cdot 66$, or $-22 = 44$

Thus, she still has 44 questions left to complete.

195. **d.** First Evelyn gave A.J. $\frac{1}{4}$ of her paycheck, so she had $\frac{3}{4}$ of her paycheck left at this point. Next, she spent $\frac{1}{3}$ of the paycheck on Jim, so we subtract $\frac{1}{3}$: $\frac{3}{4} - \frac{1}{3} = \frac{9}{12} - \frac{4}{12} = \frac{5}{12}$.

196. **d.** $\frac{1}{4}$ of the $680 bill was for oil heating. Remember that "of" means *times*. $\frac{1}{4} \cdot 680 = \frac{680}{4}$, choice **d**.

197. **c.** He addressed 14 envelopes so far, and thus has $42 - 14 = 28$ envelopes left to address. The fraction left is $\frac{28}{42} = \frac{2}{3}$.

198. **b.** Samantha ate $\frac{1}{3}$, so $1 - \frac{1}{3} = \frac{2}{3}$ was left. Then, Melissa got her hands on it and ate $\frac{1}{4}$ of that $\frac{2}{3}$, so another $\frac{1}{4} \cdot \frac{2}{3} = \frac{1}{6}$ disappeared. So we take the $\frac{2}{3}$ that was left after Samantha had some and subtract the $\frac{1}{6}$ that Melissa ate: $\frac{2}{3} - \frac{1}{6} = \frac{4}{6} - \frac{1}{6} = \frac{3}{6}$ $= \frac{1}{2}$ the pizza remains.

199. **a.** Pouring out $\frac{1}{3}$ of the mixture leaves 2 quarts inside the container. Since we know that this is a 50-50 mixture, there must be 1 qt. of juice present at this point. If we add another quart of juice, there will be 1 qt. + 1 qt. = 2 qt. juice in the final mixture.

200. **c.** At 1 o'clock, $\frac{2}{5}$ had been given out, so $\frac{3}{5}$ remained. At 3 o'clock, $\frac{1}{3}$ of the $\frac{3}{5}$ was distributed, so $\frac{1}{3} \cdot \frac{3}{5} = \frac{3}{15}$ more were given out. We subtract this $\frac{3}{15}$ from the amount that remained at 1 o'clock: $\frac{3}{5} - \frac{3}{15} = \frac{9}{15} - \frac{3}{15} = \frac{6}{15}$ remained..

201. **c.** Fractional parts are represented as $\frac{\text{PART}}{\text{WHOLE}}$. First, let's calculate the WHOLE. The total amount of water used per person is 3800 L + 2150 L + 550 L = 6500 L. We see that "Non-industrial" water usage constiutes a PART = 550 L out of that 6500 L total. Our $\frac{\text{PART}}{\text{WHOLE}}$ equation becomes $\frac{550}{6500}$. This reduces to $\frac{55}{650}$, and then reduces further to $\frac{11}{130}$.

202. **d.** If the industrial usage is decreased by $\frac{4}{5}$, then we know the new value is $\frac{1}{5}$ of the old value. The old value is 3800 L, and "of" means *multiply*, so we get $\frac{1}{5} \times 3800 = \frac{3800}{5} = 760$ L.

SECTION 3—DECIMALS

SET 12

203. c. Make sure you line up the decimal points and then subtract:

$$\begin{array}{r} 6.567 \\ -5.291 \\ \hline 1.276 \end{array}$$

204. b. Line up the decimal points and add:

$$\begin{array}{r} 3.411 \\ +7.83562 \\ \hline 11.24662 \end{array}$$

205. b. Line up the decimal points and subtract:

$$\begin{array}{r} 563.9817 \\ -61.935 \\ \hline 502.0467 \end{array}$$

206. c. Line up the decimal points and add:

$$\begin{array}{r} .24 \\ .75 \\ .89 \\ +1.27 \\ \hline 3.15 \end{array}$$

207. c. When looking to the right of the decimal point, the first spot is the *tenths place*, the second spot is the *hundredths place*, the third spot is the *thousandths place*, and so forth:

units (ones)	tenths	hundredths	thousandths	ten thousandths	hundred thousandths
0.	9	6	3	5	7

Here, we are looking for a 6 in the hundredths places, which is the second spot to the right of the decimal point. Only choice **c** has a 6 in this spot: .9 **6** 357

208. a. Line up the decimal points and add:

$$\begin{array}{r} 43.071 \\ +22.823 \\ \hline 65.894 \end{array}$$

209. d. Line up the decimal points and subtract:

$$\begin{array}{r} 6.7 \\ -2.135 \\ \hline 4.565 \end{array}$$

210. b. To solve $-4.257 + .23$, realize that you are starting on the negative side of the number line and adding .23, which means you will end up at a negative value that is closer to 0 than -4.257.

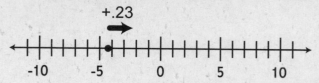

To find out exactly what that value will be, you simply subtract .23 from 4.257 and mark your answer as negative:

$$\begin{array}{r} 4.257 \\ .23 \\ \hline -4.027 \end{array}$$

211. c. Line up the decimal points and subtract:

$$\begin{array}{r} 18.731 \\ -2.04 \\ \hline 16.691 \end{array}$$

212. a. Line up the decimal points and add:

$$
\begin{array}{r}
25.25 \\
301.03 \\
4.001 \\
152 \\
+3.414 \\
\hline
485.695
\end{array}
$$

213. d. When multiplying with decimals, first you multiply in the usual fashion: .532 × .89 = 47348. Next, we need to insert the decimal point in the correct position.

.532	the decimal point is **3** places to the left
.89	the decimal point is **2** places to the left
in the answer	the decimal point should be **3 + 2**, or **5** places to the left

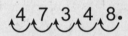

Thus, the answer is .47348

214. b. When multiplying with decimals, we first multiply in the usual fashion: 3.02 × 4.1 = 12382. Next, we need to insert the decimal point in the correct position.

3.02	the decimal point is **2** places to the left
4.1	the decimal point is **1** place to the left
in the answer	the decimal point should be **2+1**, or **3** places to the left

1 2 3 8 2.

Thus, the answer is 12.382

215. c. First multiply in the usual fashion: 7.12 × 3 = 2136. Next, we need to insert the decimal point in the correct position.

7.12	the decimal point is **2** places to the left
3	ignore whole numbers
in the answer	the decimal point should be **2** places to the left

2 1 3 6.

Thus, the answer is 21.36

216. d. Multiply in the usual fashion, and insert the decimal point 4 places to the left: .21 × .11 = .0231

217. a. Multiply in the usual fashion, and insert the decimal point 4 places to the left: 0.13 × 0.62 = .0806 = 0.0806, choice **a**.

218. b. Point A is halfway between −2 and −3, so it must be at $-2\frac{1}{2}$. Another way to write $-2\frac{1}{2}$ is −2.5, choice **b**.

SET 13

219. c. It is easiest to determine which fraction is the largest by converting them all to decimals. $\frac{12}{25} = 12 \div 25 = .48$; $\frac{11}{30} = 11 \div 30 = .366666$ repeating; $\frac{9}{15} = 9 \div 15 = .6$; and $\frac{4}{11} = 4 \div 11 = .363636$ repeating. Thus, choice **c**, $\frac{9}{15}$ is the largest.

220. **c.** When rounding to the nearest hundredth, you need to cut the number short, leaving the last digit in the hundredths place. If the number after it is a 5 or higher, you would round up.

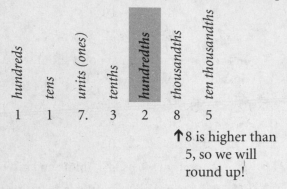

hundreds	tens	units (ones)	tenths	hundredths	thousandths	ten thousandths
1	1	7.	3	2	8	5

↑8 is higher than 5, so we will round up!

Thus, the answer is 117.33

221. **d.** .052 > .0052 because when analyzing .052, the 5 is in the *hundredths place* as compared with the 5 in the *thousandths place* in .0052. Another way to look at it is: $.052 = \frac{52}{1000}$ and $.0052 = \frac{52}{10,000}$, so .052 is obviously larger. When inserting greater than and less than symbols, the symbol should open towards the larger value: .052 > .0052

222. **c.** .071 > .0071 because a 7 in the hundredths place (.0**7**1) is greater than a 7 in the thousandths place (.00**7**1). The inequality symbol opens towards the larger value.

223. **d.** 0.005 is the same as five thousandths:

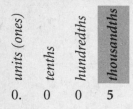

units (ones)	tenths	hundredths	thousandths
0.	0	0	5

224. **a.** When rounding to the nearest tenth, you need to cut the number short, leaving the last digit in the tenths place. If the number in the hundredths place was 5 or higher, we would round up.

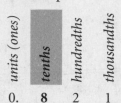

units (ones)	tenths	hundredths	thousandths
0.	8	2	1

We won't round because 2 is less than 5.

Thus, the answer is .8

225. **b.** We need a number between −.01 and 1.01. The number must be greater than −.01 and less than 1.01. Let's look at all of the choices:

Choice **a**: −.015 vs. −.01. −.015 is the same as $-\frac{15}{1000}$, and −.01 is the same as $-\frac{1}{100}$, or $-\frac{10}{1000}$, so −.015 is less than .01. This choice is *not* correct.

Choice **b**: −.005 is the same as $-\frac{5}{1000}$ which is greater than $-\frac{10}{1000}$ (−.01); therefore, −.005 is obviously less than 1.01, so this choice is correct.

Choice **c**: 1.5 is greater than 1.01, and thus is out of the range specified. This choice is *not* correct.

Choice **d**: 1.15 is also greater than 1.01, and thus is out of the range specified as well. This choice is *not* correct.

226. **b.** $\frac{5}{8} = .625$ and $\frac{2}{5} = .4$
Subtracting, .625 − .4 = .225

227. **c.** Eight and seven thousandths is the same as 8.007

units (ones)	tenths	hundredths	thousandths
8.	0	0	7

228. **d.** 5.0127 has a 7 in the ten-thousandths place:

units (ones)	tenths	hundredths	thousandths	ten-thousandths
5.	0	1	2	7

229. **c.** When rounding, we need to raise the 7 that is currently in the hundredths place to an 8 because the value in the thousandths place is 5.

units (ones)	tenths	hundredths	thousandths
0.	4	7	5

We round up because there is a 5 here.

Thus, the answer is .48

230. **c.** 1.2 > .43, because 1.2 is larger than .43, or $\frac{43}{100}$.

231. **c.** $\frac{6}{7}$ = .8571428, which, when rounded to the nearest hundredth, is .86; we round up at the hundredths spot because the number in the thousandths place is ≥ to 5.

232. **a.** The chart below shows the names of each place:

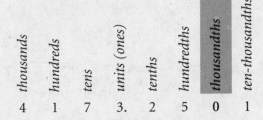

thousands	hundreds	tens	units (ones)	tenths	hundredths	thousandths	ten-thousandths
4	1	7	3.	2	5	0	1

233. **b.** Choice **b** has the 8 in the thousandths place, and is thus the smallest. The chart below shows the fractional equivalents of each choice:

a. .089 $\frac{89}{1000}$

b. .0089 $\frac{89}{10,000}$

c. .89 $\frac{89}{100}$

d. .809 $\frac{809}{1000}$

234. **b.** $\frac{31}{50}$ can quickly be converted to a fraction with a denominator (bottom) of 100 by multiplying by $\frac{2}{2}$: $\frac{31}{50} \cdot \frac{2}{2} = \frac{62}{100}$, which is the same as 62 *hundredths*, or .62.

235. **c.** 67.3**8**902 has an 8 in the hundredths place. Because the number in the thousandths place, the 9, is ≥ 5, we round up: 67.38

236. **c.** 3.830 has the greatest value because out of all the choices; it has the largest number in the tenths place:

a. 3.**0**83

b. 3.**3**08

c. 3.**8**30

d. 3.**0**38

SET 14

237. **a.** First multiply as usual: 17.12 × 34.15 = 5846480. Next, insert the decimal point 4 places to the left: 584.6480 = 584.648, choice **a.**

238. **b.** All of the answers are 3.21 times some power of 10. What do you multiply 3.21 by to make it equivalent to .0000321? It will not be choice **c** ($\times 10^6$) or **d** ($\times 10^5$) because these numbers will be bigger than 3.21 (10^6 = 1,000,000 and 10^5 = 100,000). We can turn 3.21 into .0000321 by multiplying by 10^{-5}. Thus, **b**, 3.21×10^{-5}, is the correct choice. Note that the 10^{-5} means that we will be moving the decimal place in 3.21 over five places to the left:

$$0\,.\,0\,.\,0\,.\,0\,.\,3\,.\,21$$

239. **c.** When dividing 3.09×10^{12} by 3, you just need to divide the 3.09 by 3. Thus, the answer is 1.03×10^{12}. Remember that 3.09×10^{12} is another way of expressing 3,090,000,000,000. If you divided this huge number by 3, you would get 1,030,000,000,000, which equals 1.03×10^{12}. Do not be fooled by answer choice **a**, you do not divide the exponent by 3!

240. **a.** When multiplying by a positive power of 10, just move the decimal point over to the right. Here, 10 is raised to the 4th power, so we will move the decimal point over 4 places:

$$6\,.\,2\,2\,0\,0$$

241. **d.** First, set up your division problem. Notice how you need to move the decimal point over to the right 3 places in both the divisor and dividend:

$$.0\,5\,6\,\overline{)\,1\,6\,8\,.\,0\,0\,0}$$

Next, divide as usual to get 3,000.

Note: An alternative way to look at this problem is to appreciate that $168 \div .056 = 168 \div \frac{56}{1,000} = 168 \times \frac{1,000}{56} = \frac{168,000}{56} = 3,000$.

242. **c.** First, we'll set up the division problem. Notice how we need to move the decimal point over to the right 3 places in both the divisor and dividend:

$$.0\,3\,8\,\overline{)\,.\,2\,0\,9}$$

Next, divide as usual to get 5.5

243. **a.** First, we'll set up the division problem. We need to move the decimal point one place over to the right for both the divisor and dividend:

$$3\,.\,5\,\overline{)\,7\,0\,.\,0}$$

Next, divide as usual to get 20.

244. **c.** First, we'll set up the division problem. We need to move the decimal point two places to the right for both the divisor and dividend:

$$.3\,1\,\overline{)\,1\,.\,5\,5}$$

Next, divide as usual to get 5.

245. **b.** Notice that you can cancel and reduce:

$$\frac{2.3 \times 10^{4}}{1.15 \times 10^{84}} = \frac{2.3}{1.15 \times 10^{4}}$$

If you are unfamiliar with the rules of dealing with exponents and *powers*, look at the expression written longhand below:

$$\frac{2.3 \times 10 \times 10 \times 10 \times 10}{1.15 \times 10 \times 10 \times 10 \times 10 \times 10 \times 10 \times 10 \times 10}$$

When you cross out four tens in the numerator and denominator, you are left with

$$\frac{2.3}{1.15 \times 10^{4}}$$

You divide 2.3 by 1.15 to get 2, so the expression simplifies to:

$$\frac{2}{10^{4}} = 2 \times 10^{-4}$$

A number raised to a positive power in the denominator can be rewritten as that same number to a negative power in the numerator.

246. a. To solve $(3.2 \times 10^{-3})(2.4 \times 10^5)$, we first add the exponents on the tens $(-3 + 5)$: $3.2 \times 2.4 \times 10^2 = 7.68 \times 10^2$.

247. d. When multiplying by a negative power of ten, such as 10^{-5}, you must move the decimal point over to the *left*. In this case, we move the decimal point 5 places over to the left because 10 is raised to the **negative 5th power**:

$$0\,0\,0\,0\,5.4\,3\,2\,1$$

Thus, the answer is .000054321

248. d. When multiplying by a positive power of ten, such as 10^3, you must move the decimal point over to the *right*. Thus, 1.43×10^3 can be rewritten as:

$$1.4\,3\,0$$

= 1430.

249. b. First, combine the exponents. When dividing powers of the same base (here the base is 10), we subtract the exponents (in this case $-2 - 5$, which equals -7) to rewrite the base to a new power. Thus

$$\frac{6.6 \times 10^{-2}}{3.3 \times 10^5} = \frac{6.6 \times 10^{-7}}{3.3}$$

Now we can divide 6.6 by 3.3 to get 2. So the answer is 2×10^{-7}.

SET 15

250. b. Divide the total, $27.90, by 6 students: $27.90 ÷ 6 = $4.65.

251. c. To find the total, add all of the values: $14.50 + $4.25 + $22.80 + $32.60 = $74.15.

252. b. Six bags covered an area of 315.6 square feet, so divide 315.6 by 6 to see what area one bag covered: $315.6 ÷ 6 = 52.6$

253. c. $480.85 ÷ 4 = $120.2125; because we are answering to the nearest cent, we need to cut this value short at the *hundredths* place. Because the number in the thousandths place is not ≥ 5, we get $120.21.

254. d. Every day she spends $1.52 + $1.75 + $1 = $4.27. She works 5 days a week times 4 weeks, or 20 days. We multiply $4.27 × 20 = $85.40.

255. a. There are 2.54 cm. in an inch. A yard has $\frac{12''}{ft.} \times 3$ ft. $= 36''$. We multiply $\frac{2.54\text{ cm.}}{in.} \times \frac{36\text{ in.}}{yd.}$ to get $\frac{2.54 \times 36\text{ cm.}}{yd.}$

256. b. The total amount earned in tips is: $50.34 + $63.25 + $44.30 = $157.89. Divided among 3 workers, we get: $157.89 ÷ 3 = $52.63.

257. b. $4.52 - .02 = 4.5$ and $4.52 + .02 = 4.54$; thus, an acceptable answer must be between 4.5 and 4.54, inclusive. Choice **b**, Anthony (4.51) is the only value within this acceptable range.

Student	Mass calculated
Brian	4.55
Anthony	**4.51**
Danielle	4.32
Vincent	4.02

258. c. We will set up a proportion. It costs $1.25 per 100 count for paper clips and we want to know how much it will cost for 556 paper clips.

$$\frac{\$1.25}{100\text{ clips}} = \frac{?}{556\text{ clips}}$$

Note that only choice **c** is equivalent to this proportion. Choice **a** uses "125" which would solve for *cents*, not *dollars*.

259. a. $6\frac{1}{2}$ pounds = 6.5 pounds. We multiply: 6.5 lbs. $\times \frac{\$1.50}{\text{lb.}}$ = \$9.75.

260. c. First, subtract the weight of the crate from the total. 192 lbs. − 14.5 lbs. = 177.5 lbs. Next, divide this weight by the weight of one book to see how many books there are: 177.5 ÷ 1.25 = 142.

SET 16

261. d. Here, we subtract: 45.2 − 43.7 = 1.5 g.

262. a. The total amount that she needs is $\frac{\$2.45}{\text{lb.}} \times$ 8 lbs. = \$19.60. She already has \$13.45, so she needs \$19.60 − \$13.45 = \$6.15 more.

263. c. First, notice that the series is decreasing. From 8.60 to 8.45, we decreased by .15; now, look at the other end of the series. From 8.15 to 8, we also decreased by .15; to fill in the blank, we subtract: 8.45 − .15 = 8.3

264. b. We multiply 3.52 boxes $\times \frac{100\text{ fasteners}}{\text{box}}$ = 352 fasteners.

265. d. We set up a proportion:

$$\frac{\$5.49}{30\text{ salads}} = \frac{?\text{ dollars}}{11\text{ salads}}$$

Cross multiplying, we get: 5.49 · 11 = 30 · ?, which is the same as 60.39 = 30 · ?. Dividing both sides by 30, we get 2.013 = ?, so we round this answer off to \$2.00, choice **d**.

266. c. Arranging these in order from least to greatest, we get: 5.003, 5.025, 5.03, 5.12, 5.251. The number 5.003 has a 3 in the thousandths place and only zeroes in the hundredths and tenths place. Next, 5.025 has a 2 in the hundredths place. After that, 5.03 is the next greatest with a 3 in the hundredths place. Then we have 5.12, which has a one in the tenths place, followed by 5.251 which has a two in the tenths place.

267. a. Here we add: 8.25 lbs. + 10.4 lbs. + 7.5 lbs. + 6.25 lbs. = 32.4 lbs.

268. b. \$15.99 + \$13.99 + \$12.99 + \$25.44 + \$45.59 + \$9.44 = \$123.44, total. She pays with three fifty-dollar bills, or \$150. Her change will be \$150 − \$123.44 = \$26.56.

Here's a trick: When adding \$15.99 + \$13.99 + \$12.99, just add 16 + 14 + 13 and subtract 3¢.

269. d. Cost per pound would be $\frac{\$}{\text{lb.}}$, so we divide: $\frac{\$3.00}{25}$ = .12

270. b. For the beef: 1.5 lbs. $\times \frac{5{,}214\text{ gal}}{\text{lb.}}$ = 7,821 gallons. For the tomatoes: 150 lbs. $\times \frac{23\text{ gal}}{\text{lb.}}$ = 3450 gallons. The difference is: 7,821 − 3450 = 4,371 gallons.

271. c. We add: 8 + (2 × 25) + (3 × 7.5) = 8 + 50 + 22.5 = 80.5 pounds.

272. a. Average = $\frac{\text{sum of all values}}{\text{number of values}}$. In this case, average = $\frac{72}{5}$ = 14.4 rooms.

273. d. Ed started with \$100, and he spent \$6.25 + \$13.75 + \$48.40 = \$68.40. This means he has \$100 − \$68.40 = \$31.60 left.

274. b. To solve this question, we set up a proportion:

$$\frac{100\text{ staples}}{2\text{ in.}} = \frac{1\text{ staple}}{?\text{ in.}}$$

Cross multiply to get: 100 · ? = 2. Divide both sides by 100 to yield ? = 2 ÷ 100 = .02 in.

275. a. For the gel pens, she spends: \$3.50 × 3 = \$10.50. For the felt-tip pens, she spends \$2.75 × 2 = \$5.50. Altogether, she spends: \$10.50 + \$5.50 = \$16.00.

SET 17

276. **c.** Each hour, the level of the water increases by .21 cm. Let's add data for 8 A.M., 9 A.M., and 10 A.M. in the chart below:

Time	Water Height
5 A.M.	23.02 cm
6 A.M.	23.23 cm
7 A.M.	23.44 cm
8 A.M.	23.65 cm
9 A.M.	23.86 cm
10 A.M.	24.07 cm

Thus, at 10 A.M., the height will be 24.07 cm.

277. **a.** Separately, the cost of the 4 listed items would be: $252.49 + $149.99 + $152.49 + $499.99 = $1,054.96. The difference between this amount and the cost of the All-In-One machine is: $1,054.96 − $799.99 = $254.97. Notice that the answer choices include numbers that are spread out:

a. $254.97
b. $302.57
c. $404.96
d. $1,054.96

Thus, you needn't worry about the tedious decimal calculations. If you approximate the values, you'd get a total of $252 + $150 + $152 + $500 = $1,054 for the purchase of the separate machines. Then you'd subtract $1,054 − $800 = $254, and you'd pick choice **a**.

278. **c.** To find the average, you use the following formula:

$$Average\ (mean) = \frac{sum\ of\ all\ values}{\#\ of\ values}$$

Here we know the average is $18.95, and that the number of values = 4 (there are 4 books). Substituting, we get:

$$\$18.95 = \frac{sum\ of\ all\ values}{4}$$

Cross-multiplying, we get $18.95 • 4 = *sum of all values*, which means $75.80 = *sum of all values*. So, the four books totaled $75.80, and we know the price of three of these books. Therefore, we can subtract the price of the three books to find out the cost of the fourth: $75.80 − $25.25 − $14.95 − $19.95 = $15.65.

279. **d.** There were four envelopes with an undisclosed amount of money inside:

Then, Clarissa came along and gave one away. We know that there is a total of $71.25 in the remaining three envelopes.

$71.25 total ÷ 3 envelopes = $23.75 in each

Now we know that each envelope has $23.75 enclosed. Therefore, the four envelopes had a total of $23.75 × 4 = $95.

280. **b.** The first stone weighs 48.3 lbs., and the second weighs $\frac{1}{3}$ • 48.3 = 16.1 lbs. Thus, combined, they weigh 48.3 lbs. + 16.1 lbs. = 64.4 lbs.

281. **d.** Here, we can set up a proportion:

$$\frac{250\ pieces}{.5\ in.} = \frac{1\ piece}{?\ in.}$$

Cross multiplying, we get: 250 • ? = .5 • 1, which means 250 • ? = .5; dividing both sides by 250, we get ? = .5 ÷ 250 = .002 in.

282. **d.** She drove 75 miles, and she gets $\frac{25\ mi.}{gal.}$, so she used $\frac{75\ miles \times 1\ gal.}{25\ mi.}$ = 3 gallons of gas. Notice that when making the conversion factor, we put the units that we wanted to cross out (miles) in the denominator (bottom), so that the resulting answer was in gallons. Next, we multiply the number of gallons by the cost per gallon: 3 gal. × \$1.65 = \$4.95.

283. **a.** Divide the total weight by 6 to get the weight of 1 wedge: 30.48 ÷ 6 = 5.08 g.

284. **c.** We know that 12 inches = 1 foot. This means that $(1 \text{ ft.})^3 = (12 \text{ in.})^3 = 1728 \text{ in.}^3$ We also know that ice weighs $\frac{.033 \text{ lb.}}{\text{in.}^3}$ so we multiply: $\frac{.033 \text{ lb.}}{\text{in.}^3} \times \frac{1728 \text{ in.}^3}{\text{ft.}^3} = \frac{57.024 \text{ lbs.}}{\text{ft.}^3}$.

285. **c.** First, plan your strategy carefully. Do you really want to do calculations that involve the range .148–.181? Didn't think so. So let's ignore the weight range for pyrite and test to see if the blocks are pure gold. Pure gold always weighs $\frac{.698 \text{ lbs.}}{\text{in.}^3}$. The volume of Block A is V = 2 × 4 × 5 = 40 in.^{3} To see if Block A is pure gold we multiply: $40 \text{ in.}^3 \times \frac{.698 \text{ lbs.}}{\text{in.}^3} = 27.92$ lbs. Block A does, in fact, weigh 27.92 lbs., so it *is* pure gold. Now, we look at Block B: V = 2 × 8 × 1 = 16 in.^{3} If this were pure gold, it would weigh $16 \text{ in.}^3 \times \frac{.698 \text{ lbs.}}{\text{in.}^3} = 11.168$ lbs. Block B doesn't weigh 11.168 lbs., and therefore *is not* pure gold.

286. **c.** The scale is $\frac{1}{4}$ in. = 1 mile, or .25 in. = 1 mile, so we set up a proportion:

$$\frac{.25 \text{ in.}}{1 \text{ mile}} = \frac{5.75 \text{ in.}}{? \text{ miles}}$$

Cross multiply to get: .25 • ? = 1 • 5.75, or .25 • ? = 5.75; then we divide both sides by .25 to get $? = \frac{5.75}{.25} = 23$ miles.

SECTION 4—PERCENTS

SET 18

287. **b.** When you see a percent symbol, %, you just move the decimal point 2 places to the left. Thus, 35% = .35.

288. **d.** When you see a percent symbol, %, you can rewrite the percent as a fraction by placing the value at 100. Thus, $52\% = \frac{52}{100}$. Because $\frac{52}{100}$ is not an answer choice, reduce to $\frac{13}{25}$.

289. **c.** When written as fractions, percents have a denominator of 100. We can easily convert $\frac{42}{50}$ to a fraction with a denominator of 100 by multiplying by $\frac{2}{2}$. $\frac{42}{50} \times \frac{2}{2} = \frac{84}{100} = 84\%$.

290. **c.** First, we put 27.5 over $100 = \frac{27.5}{100}$. This is not an answer choice, so we need to reduce. In order to reduce $\frac{27.5}{100}$, it is easier to rewrite this fraction as $\frac{275}{1,000}$ (we multiplied top and bottom by 10). Now we reduce $\frac{275}{1,000} = \frac{55}{200} = \frac{11}{40}$.

291. **c.** We need to find 17%, or .17 of 3,400. Remember that *of* means *multiply*: .17 × 3,400 = 578.

292. **d.** We need to get the value $\frac{3}{45}$ into the form of *hundredths*. We can divide: 3 ÷ 45 = .0666666. .0666666 = 6.66666% = $6\frac{2}{3}$%. The other option would be to take the original fraction $\frac{3}{45}$ and set up a proportion: $\frac{3}{45} = \frac{?}{100}$. We cross multiply to get 300 = 45 • ?. Thus, ? = $6\frac{2}{3}$, so the answer is $6\frac{2}{3}$%.

293. **a.** 12.5% = .125, and $\frac{3}{8}$ = .375. Therefore, .125 < .375, and choice **a** is correct.

294. **b.** You can rewrite the percent as a fraction by placing the value over 100. Thus 6.2% = $\frac{6.2}{100}$ = $\frac{62}{1000}$ = $\frac{31}{500}$.

295. **d.** It is easier to change $\frac{2}{5}$ into .4 before dealing with the percent symbol. $\frac{2}{5}$% = .4% = .004

296. **c.** We need to get the value $\frac{3}{24}$ into the form of *hundredths*. We can divide: 3 ÷ 24 = .125, and .125 = 12.5%. The other option would be to take the original fraction $\frac{3}{24}$ and set up a proportion: $\frac{3}{24} = \frac{?}{100}$. We cross multiply to get 300 = 24 • ?. Thus, ? = 12.5, so the answer is 12.5%.

297. **b.** The % symbol is equivalent to the two following actions:
- **Place the value before the % over 100.** In this case 22.5% = $\frac{22.5}{100}$ = .225
- **Take the value before the % symbol and move the decimal point 2 places to the left.** In this case, 22.5% = .225

SET 19

298. **c.** We need to find 400%, or $\frac{400}{100}$ (which is 4) of 30. Remember that *of* means *multiply*. 4 × 30 = 120.

299. **a.** We know 25% = $\frac{y}{40}$. Because 25% = .25, the equation is equivalent to .25 = $\frac{y}{40}$. Multiplying both sides by 40, we get 40 × .25 = *y*. Thus, *y* = 10.

300. **c.** Let's convert this question into a mathematical equation:

112 is 80% of which of the following numbers?

$$112 = .80 \cdot ?$$

Thus, we divide 112 by .80 to get 140.

301. **d.** *"40 percent of what number is equal to 108?"* can be written mathematically as .40 • ? = 108. Dividing both sides by .40, we get: ? = 270.

302. **a.** We know 25 percent of *x* is 23. Mathematically, we can express this as .25 • *x* = 23. Dividing both sides by .25 we get *x* = 92.

303. d. Just as you would express 5% as $\frac{5}{100}$, you can put an unknown percent over 100. Therefore, *"What percentage"* can be expressed mathematically as $\frac{?}{100}$. This means that the question *"What percentage of 40 is 32?"* can be expressed as: $\frac{?}{100} \cdot 40 = 32$. Thus, $\frac{40 \cdot ?}{100} = 32$

Cross multiplying, we get $40 \cdot ? = 3200$. Dividing both sides by 40 yields $? = 80$. Therefore 32 is 80% of 40.

304. c. *"What percentage"* can be expressed mathematically as $\frac{?}{100}$. The question *"What percent of $\frac{8}{9}$ is $\frac{1}{3}$?"* can be expressed as: $\frac{?}{100} \cdot \frac{8}{9} = \frac{1}{3}$, which is the same as

$$\frac{8 \cdot ?}{900} = \frac{1}{3}$$

Cross multiplying, we get $3 \cdot 8 \cdot ? = 900$, or $24 \cdot ? = 900$. Dividing both sides by 24, we get 37.5; thus, 37.5% of $\frac{8}{9}$ is $\frac{1}{3}$.

305. b. *"What percentage of 300 is 400?"* can be written as $\frac{?}{100} \cdot 300 = 400$, or

$$\frac{300 \cdot ?}{100} = 400.$$

Notice that we can reduce:

$$\frac{\overset{3}{\cancel{300}} \cdot ?}{\cancel{100}} = 400.$$

So, $3 \cdot ? = 400$, and $? = 133\frac{1}{3}\%$

SET 20

306. d. $25\% = \frac{25}{100}$. This reduces to $\frac{1}{4}$. Taking $\frac{1}{4}$ of a dollar amount means you multiply the dollar amount by $\frac{1}{4}$, which is the same as dividing by 4.

307. c. Lauren, Jenna, and Rich sold 40%, 15%, and 30%. When combined, these add to 85%.

308. c. "20% of \$325" is the same as $.20 \times 325$. This is not an answer choice, so you have to look to see which choice expresses the same amount. Choice **c**, $2 \times .10(325) = .20 \times 325$.

309. d. The enrollment is increased by 75%, so the amount of the increase is $\frac{3}{4}E$. Add this amount to the initial enrollment to find the new enrollment: $E + \frac{3}{4}E$.

310. c. If there is a 15% discount, then the new price will be 85% of the original, or $.85V$.

311. a. Because *percent* means "out of 100," we can set up a proportion as follows:

$$\frac{180 \text{ days}}{365 \text{ days per year}} = \frac{X}{100}$$

Thus, choice **a** is correct.

312. b. If you took 100% of a number, you would have the very same number. Taking 150% of a number will give you a *larger* number. In fact, taking 150% of a number yields a number that is 50% larger than the original.

313. b. 7% of the 4,700 men would be expected to be colorblind. Thus, we predict that $.07 \times 4,700 = 329$ men are colorblind. Also, 1% of the 4,900 women, or $.01 \times 4,900 = 49$ women are expected to be colorblind. We would therefore predict that $329 + 49 = 378$ people are colorblind in Mastic.

314. a. There is a 15% discount, so the final price will be 85% of the usual price. The usual (non-discounted) price is $W + X + Y + Z$. To take 85% of this amount, we multiply by .85: $.85(W + X + Y + Z)$, choice **a**.

315. c. "Car" represents 12%, "food" represents 21%, and "recreation" represents 17%. In adding these three values up, you get $12\% + 21\% + 17\% = 50\%$, which is $\frac{50}{100}$, or $\frac{1}{2}$ his expenses.

316. d. Food represents 21% of his total monthly expenses. We need to find 21% of $1,500. Mathematically, 21% = .21, and "of" means *multiply*. (.21)($1500) = $315 a month spent on food. Remember that the question asks for the amount spent on food over the course of *two* months. This means we double the $315, so $315 × 2 = $630.

317. b. Percents are always *out of 100*. The chart even reminds you that the total is 100%. This means that 18% + 10% + 65% + x% = 100%. You get: x = 100 − 18 − 10 − 65 = 7. Thus, x = 7.

318. a. To calculate the percent increase, use this proportion:

$$\frac{change}{initial} = \frac{I}{100}$$

First, calculate the *change* by looking at the graph. Note that the white bars represent "Oil."

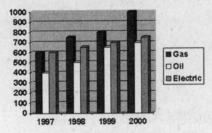

The cost rose from the *initial* $400 in 1997 to $500 in 1998. So, the *change* was $100. Thus, we get:

$$\frac{100}{400} = \frac{I}{100}$$

Cross-multiplying, we get: 100 · 100 = 400I, or 10,000 = 400I, and dividing both sides by 400 yields I = 25. This means the percent increase was 25%.

319. c. Use the chart to note that "Overseas" brought in 9% of the total. We know the total is $270,000, so we take 9% of this amount: .09 × $270,000 = $24,300.

320. a. Use the chart to figure out what the second quotes are:

	Original Quote	Second Quote	
K Tech	$12,000	decrease original quote by $\frac{1}{4}$	$12,000 − $\frac{1}{4}$($12,000) = $9,000
L Tech	$13,400	75% of original quote	.75 × $13,400 = $10,050
M Tech	$11,500	less 15% from original quote	$11,500 − .15($11,500) = $9,775
N Tech	$15,000	$\frac{7}{8}$ of original offer	$\frac{7}{8}$ × $15,000 = $13,125

Thus, the best price is K Tech's quote of $9,000.

SET 21

321. d. Management represents 20% of the staff. The total staff is 18,950, so we take 20% of 18,950: .20 × 18,950 = 3,790.

322. d. To calculate the percent increase, use this proportion:

$$\frac{change}{initial} = \frac{I}{100}$$

First, calculate the *change* by looking at the graph. Note that the black bars represent "Charge Card Interest."

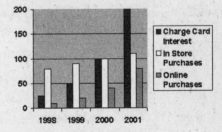

Thus, the *initial* value is 50 (in 1999) and the value in 2001 was 200. The *change* is then 200 − 50 = 150.

$\frac{change}{initial} = \frac{I}{100}$ becomes $\frac{150}{50} = \frac{I}{100}$

Cross-multiplying we get $100 \cdot 150 = 50I$, or $15,000 = 50I$, and dividing both sides by 50 yields $I = 300$. Thus, there was a 300% increase.

323. d. The stocks averaged \$12.45 per share for April. In May, the stocks averaged 14% higher, so we add $.14 \times 12.45$ to original price:

$$12.45 + .14(12.45)$$

Thus, choice **c** is true. Notice that this can be simplified:

$$1(12.45) + .14(12.45) = 1.14(1.45)$$

Thus, choice **b** is also true, and the answer is then choice **d**.

324. b. We set up the proportion as follows:

$$\frac{4 \text{ days}}{7 \text{ days per week}} = \frac{x}{100}$$

Thus, choice **b** is correct.

325. d. The meals will cost $(a + b + c)$ dollars. To that cost, a 15% tip will be added in. This tip equals $.15(a + b + c)$. The entire cost is then $(a + b + c) + .15(a + b + c)$. This gets divided by 2 brothers:

$$\frac{(a + b + c) + .15(a + b + c)}{2}$$

Thus, choice **c** is true. Note that this equation can be simplified to:

$$\frac{1.15(a + b + c)}{2}$$

Thus, choice **b** is also true. The correct answer is **d**.

326. c. We need to subtract 15% of \$448, or $.15(448)$ from the original price (\$448): $448 - .15(\$448)$. Thus, choice **c** is correct.

327. c. The formula $I = PRT$ means:

Interest = principal $\times$ rate of interest $\times$ time

Principal = your original amount of money (in dollars), and *time* is in *years*.

In this question, $P = \$3,200$, $R = 8\%$, or $.08$, and $I = \$768$. Substituting into the equation, we get: $\$768 = \$3200 \times .08 \times T$, or $\$768 = 256T$, and dividing both sides by 256 yields $T = 3$. Thus, the time = 3 years.

328. a. The formula $I = PRT$ means:

Interest = principal $\times$ rate of interest $\times$ time

Where *principal* = your original amount of money (in dollars), and *time* is in *years*. Here, we were given the time frame of 8 months, so we need to convert to years. 8 months $\times \frac{1 \text{ yr}}{12 \text{ months}}$ $= \frac{8}{12}$ yr. $= \frac{2}{3}$ yr. We are given $P = \$10,000$ and $R = 6\%$ or $.06$. Next, we substitute these values into the equation:

$$I = PRT$$
$$I = (\$10,000)(.06)\left(\tfrac{2}{3}\right)$$
$$= 600 \times \tfrac{2}{3}$$
$$= \tfrac{1,200}{3}$$
$$= \$400$$

329. d. We need to take V and add 25% of V. 25% $= .25$ or $\frac{25}{100} = \frac{1}{4}$. Thus, choice **a**, $V + \frac{1}{4}V$ is true. This is the same as $V + .25V$, which is choice **c**. Choice **c** can be simplified to $1.25V$, which is choice **b**.

330. b. To calculate the percent increase, use this proportion:

$$\frac{change}{initial} = \frac{I}{100}$$

Here, the *change* is $366 - 331 = 35$, and the *initial* value was 331. Substituting, we get:
$\frac{35}{331} = \frac{I}{100}$

SET 22

331. b. 15% of 360 is .15 times 360: .15 × 360 = 54.

332. a. The question: "40% of what number is equal to 230?" can be written mathematically as: .40 × *?* = 230. We divide both sides by .40 to yield *?* = 575.

333. d. .23 × 441 = 101.43

334. c. 8% of 5% of 4,000 = .08 × .05 × 4,000 = 16.

335. c. If 60 of the 750 are damaged, then 750 − 60 = 690 must be in good condition. We set up a proportion: $\frac{690}{750} = \frac{?}{100}$. Cross-multiplying, we get 690 · 100 = 750 · *?*, or 69,000 = 750 · *?*. Dividing both sides by 750 yields *?* = 92. Thus, 92% are in good condition.

336. d. He gets 12% of $4,000, or .12 × $4,000 = $480.

337. b. Of the total bill of $540, Erika paid 30% or $540 × .30 = $162. This means that she still needs to pay $540 − $162 = $378.

338. b. If she took out 15% of her money, she must have 85% of her money still in the account. 85% of what initial amount is equal to $12,070? We can express this question mathematically as: .85 · *?* = $12,070. Dividing both sides by .85 yields *?* = $14,200.

339. c. There will be a discount on this purchase because more that 100 kits are being ordered. We can take 20% off of the regular price of $6 to see how much each kit will cost: .20 × $6 = $1.20 is discounted. Thus, each kit costs $6 − $1.20 = $4.80. Next, we multiply the price by the number being purchased: $4.80 × 150 = $720.

340. d. To find the percentage, set up a proportion: $\frac{1}{250,000} = \frac{?}{100}$. We cross-multiply to get 100 = 250,000 · *?*, and we divide both sides by 250,000 to yield *?* = .0004%.

341. a. 330 with black logo + 170 with the blue logo = 500 total were given out. The percent that had the blue logo would then be $\frac{170}{500}$ = 170 ÷ 500 = .34 which is the decimal form of 34%.

342. a. From the $42,500, we deduct 14.5%, or .145 × $42,500 = $6,162.50. Thus, the net amount would be $42,500 − $6,162.50 = $36,337.50.

343. b. Look at the chart to see that "Car" represents 15% of the total $2,000 per month. 15% of $2,000 = .15 × $2000 = $300.

344. d. This question is really asking: "$450,000 is 125% of what number?" Mathematically, we'd write: $450,000 = 1.25 × *?*. Dividing both sides by 1.25, we get *?* = $360,000.

345. b. Cash Prize − .40(*Cash Prize*) = $18,000. Thus, .60(*Cash Prize*) = $18,000. Dividing both sides by .60 yields: *Cash Prize* = $18,000 ÷ .60 = $30,000.

346. a. Use the chart to note that the programming staff represents 13% of the total staff at Drake Technologies. We take 13% of the 1,400 total: .13 × 1,400 = 182.

347. a. Jack needs to get 80% of 65 correct. 80% of 65 = .80 × 65, choice a.

348. b. He put away 120 out of a total of 800. We can set up a proportion to see what this would be equivalent to "out of 100."

$$\frac{120}{800} = \frac{?}{100}$$

Cross-multiplying, we get 120 · 100 = 800 × *?*, which is the same as 12,000 = 800 × *?*, and dividing both sides by 800 yields $? = 15$. Thus, he put away 15%.

349. **c.** Ultimately, he scores on 90% of his shots:

$$\frac{shots\ made}{shots\ attempted} = \frac{90}{100}$$

Throughout the game his total amount of baskets made would be 15 in the first half plus m in the second half.

$$\frac{15 + m}{shots\ attempted} = \frac{90}{100}$$

Also, throughout the game he attempted a total of 20 shots in the first half plus m shots in the second half.

$$\frac{15 + m}{20 + m} = \frac{90}{100}$$

We cross-multiply to get: $100 \cdot (15 + m) = 90 \cdot (20 + m)$. Distributing, we get: $1{,}500 + 100m = 1800 + 90m$. We subtract 1,500 from each side to yield: $100m = 300 + 90m$. Subtracting $90m$ from both sides, we get $10m = 300$. Finally, divide both sides by 10 to get $m = 30$.

350. **d.** To calculate the percent increase, use this proportion:

$$\frac{change}{initial} = \frac{I}{100}$$

Here, the *change* = $350 - 280 = 70$, and the *initial* value = 280. Substituting, we get: $\frac{70}{280} = \frac{I}{100}$. Cross-multiplying yields $100 \cdot 70 = 280 \cdot I$, or $7{,}000 = 280 \cdot I$. Dividing both sides by 280 gives us the answer: $I = 25$. Thus, there was a 25% increase in the concentration of CO_2.

351. **a.** To calculate the percent decrease, use this proportion:

$$\frac{change}{initial} = \frac{D}{100}$$

Here, the *change* is $30 - 24 = 6$, and the *initial* value is $30. Substituting these values into the formula, we get:

$$\frac{6}{30} = \frac{D}{100}$$

Cross-multiplying, we get $6 \cdot 100 = 30D$, or $600 = 30D$. Dividing both sides by 30 yields: $D = 20$. Thus, there was a 20% decrease.

352. **b.** Janice paid 15% less than the price of $1,500. Another way to look at it, is that she paid 85% of the price of $1,500. Thus, she paid $.85 \times 1{,}500 = .85(1{,}500)$, choice **b.**

353. **d.** If $\frac{1}{4}$ was consumed, then $\frac{3}{4}$ remains. Multiplying $\frac{3}{4}$ by $\frac{25}{25}$ yields $\frac{75}{100}$, which is one way of expressing 75%.

354. **b.** Note that we are only adding water to the initial 20% bleach–80% water mixture. This means that the amount of bleach is the same in both mixtures. Thus, the amount of bleach that comprised 20% of the initial 2L is the same amount of bleach present when comprising the 10% of the new $2L + ?$ mixture. If we set these values equal to each other, we can solve for the "$?$". Thus, $.20 \times 2 = .10 \times (2 + ?)$, or $.4 = .10 \times (2 + ?)$, and dividing both sides by .10 yields: $4 = 2 + ?$, so $? = 2L$.

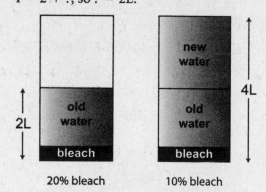

20% bleach   10% bleach

355. **d.**

$$\frac{change}{initial} = \frac{D}{100}$$

Here, the *change* is $180 - 60 = 120$, and the *initial* value is 180. Substituting these values into the formula, we get:

$$\frac{120}{180} = \frac{D}{100}$$

Cross-multiplying, we get 120 • 100 = 180*D*, or 12,000 = 180*D*. Dividing both sides by 180 yields: $D = 66\frac{2}{3}$. Thus, there was a $66\frac{2}{3}$% decrease.

356. a. Before he added the new bleach, there was 2 gal. × 30% bleach = 2 gal. × .30 = .6 gal. of bleach. After he adds the new bleach, there is 2 gal. + .5 gal. = 2.5 gallons total. There was .6 gallons of bleach before + .5 gallon of new bleach added = 1.1 gallons of bleach present in the new solution. 1.1 gallons of bleach out of a total 2.5 gallons can be expressed as a percent by dividing: 1.1 ÷ 2.5 = .44 which is one way of expressing 44%. There would then be 56% water present. If you do not like to figure out percentages by dividing, you could also make a proportion. Thus, for percent bleach:

$$\frac{1.1 \text{ gal.}}{2.5 \text{ gal}} = \frac{?}{100}$$

Cross-multiply to get 1.1 • 100 = 2.5 • *?*, or 110 = 2.5 • *?*, and dividing both sides by 2.5 yields *?* = 44%.

SECTION 5—ALGEBRA

SET 24

357. **b.** Cassie is seven years older than Elijah. This means that Elijah's age plus 7 will yield Cassie's age. Choice **b**, $E + 7 = C$, represents this statement.

$$E + 7 = C$$

means

Elijah's age + 7 = Cassie's age

358. **a.** Let's call the number N. 15 more than a number is 52, and it can be expressed as $15 + N = 52$. We subtract 15 from both sides to get $N = 37$.

359. **c.** Let's take this question piece by piece. "6 less than 6 times a number" can be expressed as: $6N - 6$.

"is equal to 5 times one more than the number" can be expressed as: $= 5(N+1)$.

Notice the use of parentheses. We are multiplying "one more than the number" by 5.

Thus, our equation is: $6N - 6 = 5(N+1)$. We distribute the 5 on the right side:

$$6N - 6 = 5(N + 1)$$

This yields $6N - 6 = 5N + 5$. Now we add 6 to both sides to get $6N = 5N + 11$. Finally, subtract $5N$ from both sides to yield $N = 11$.

360. **d.** Let's take the statement piece by piece. "A number is tripled" can be expressed as $3N$, "and then decreased by 23" is written mathematically as minus 23, or -23, "resulting in a value of 28" means equals 28, or $= 28$. Putting it all together,

we have: $3N - 23 = 28$. We add 23 to both sides to get $3N = 51$. Dividing both sides by 3 yields $N = 17$.

361. **a.** If the coordinator handed out "a tickets to b people," that means that she gave away a total of a tickets. She has c tickets left over, so she must have started with $a + c$ tickets.

362. **c.** Let's look at the given equation:

$$3x + 15 = 32$$

3 times a number   plus 15   equals 32

Thus, choice **c** is correct.

363. **c.** We multiply the number of desks (x) by the cost per desk ($\$D$) to get the total cost for all the desks: xD. We multiply the number of chairs (y) by the cost per chair ($\$E$) to get the total cost for all the desks: yE. We multiply the number of file cabinets (z) by the cost per file cabinet ($\$F$) to get the total cost for all the file cabinets: zF. Combining all of these, the total cost, $T = xD + yE + zF$.

364. **b.** The first number is a. The reciprocal of a different number is $\frac{1}{b}$. Remember that when you take the reciprocal of a number, such as the number b, you put 1 over it. The third number is c. Thus, the whole statement can be expressed as $a + \frac{1}{b} = c$.

365. **a.** The reciprocal of $\frac{2}{a}$ is $\frac{a}{2}$. We add this to $\frac{1}{2}$ to get: $\frac{a}{2} + \frac{1}{2}$. This is not an answer choice, so you need to combine $t =$ your terms. Both values have a denominator of 2. That means we can combine the numerators over this common denominator:

$$\frac{a + 1}{2}$$

SET 25

366. **d.** Let's look at the given equation:

$$3x - 8 = 25$$

Eight less than...

3 times a number...

equals 32.

Thus, choice **d** is correct.

367. **a.** "Eight times one-third of a number is thirty-two" can be expressed as $8 \times \frac{1}{3} \times N = 32$. This means $\frac{8}{3}N = 32$. Multiplying both sides by $\frac{3}{8}$, we get $N = \frac{96}{8}$, and $N = 12$.

368. **d.** Let's call the number "N." When we subtract 42 from N, we get 56. Thus $N - 42 = 56$. Adding 42 to both sides, we get: $N = 98$.

369. **b.** Pretend we are talking about money. Let's say you handed one friend $5 and another friend $13, and you were left holding $41. So, there you are, the three of you, just standing around holding money. How much did you start with? Well, you'd just add up all three handfuls of money: $5 + 13 + 41 = 59$ initially.

370. **d.** *Consecutive* means "successive" or "in a row." Let's represent our 3 consecutive odd numbers as: N, $N+2$, and $N+4$. These three will add to 99, so we have: $N + N+2 + N+4 = 99$. Combining terms we get $3N + 6 = 99$. We subtract 6 from both sides to yield $3N = 93$. Dividing both sides by 3, we get $N = 31$. But be CAREFUL! We want the *middle* number, or $N+2$, so the answer is 33.

371. **a.** Let's call the number "N." 30% of a number $= .30 \times N$. We add $.30N$ to N to yield 156. Thus, our equation looks like this: $.3N + N = 156$. We combine the $.3N$, and the $1N$ to get $1.3N = 156$. Dividing both sides by 1.3, we get $N = 120$.

372. **b.** If we call our number N, "$\frac{7}{8}$ of nine times a number" can be expressed as $\frac{7}{8} \cdot 9N$. The next part, "is equal to ten times the number minus 17," can be expressed as $= 10N - 17$. Thus, our equation is: $\frac{7}{8} \cdot 9N = 10N - 17$, or $\frac{63N}{8} = 10N - 17$. We multiply both sides by 8 to get: $63N = 8(10N - 17)$. Distributing the 8 on the right side of the equation, we get: $63N = 80N - 136$. Add 136 to both sides to yield $136 + 63N = 80N$, and then subtract $63N$ from both sides to get $136 = 17N$. Finally, divide both sides by 17 to get $N = 8$.

373. **d.** Let's call our number "N." Looking at the statement, the first part says, "Ten times 40% of a number . . ." We can express this mathematically as $10 \times .40N$. Remember that 40% is the same as .40 and "of" means *multiply*. The next part of the statement is " . . . is equal to 4 less than the product of 6 times the number." This can be expressed as $= 6N - 4$. Putting it all together, we have $10 \times .40N = 6N - 4$, or $4N = 6N - 4$. We add 4 to both sides to get $4 + 4N = 6N$. Next, subtract $4N$ from both sides to yield $4 = 2N$, thus, $N = 2$.

374. **a.** Let $N =$ the number. First look at "three is added to the product of 2 and a number." So, we have $2N + 3$. Next, we know this equals "103 minus twice the number," or $103 - 2N$. Thus, our equation is $2N + 3 = 103 - 2N$. Combining like terms, we *get* $4N = 100$, and $N = 25$.

375. **c.** Let's call the smaller number "S," and thus, the bigger number will be ($S + 15$). The sum of these 2 numbers is 63, so we have $S + (S+15) = 63$. Notice that this equation is the same as saying SMALL + BIG = 63. Next, we combine the variables to get $2S + 15 = 63$. Subtract 15 from both sides: $2S = 48$. Divide both sides by 2 to get $S = 24$.

376. **b.** We will add $11x - 3y$ and $11y - 6x$. We have:

$$11x - 3y + 11y - 6x =$$

We combine like terms to get $5x + 8y$, which is choice **b.**

SET 26

377. **b.** Looking at $x^2 - 8x$, we see that the first term (x^2) and the second term ($8x$) both are divisible by x. That means that we can "pull out" an x and place it outside of a set of parentheses, like this: $x(x - 8)$. You can check your answer by distributing the x inside the parentheses:

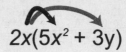

$$= x^2 - 8x.$$

378. **d.** $8x^2y^3z^5 \div 2x$ is the same as

$$\frac{8x^2y^3z^5}{2x}$$

We can cancel:

$$\frac{\overset{4}{8}x^2y^3z^5}{2x}$$

Also, when dealing with exponents, if you have the same base (in this case x is the base), and you are dividing powers of that base, you subtract the exponents. Thus, $x^2 \div x = x^2 \div x^1 = x$. So, now we have:

$$4xy^3z^5$$

379. **a.** First, we distribute the x:

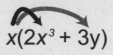

Note that when multiplying x by $2x^3$, we get $2x^4$. Thus, the expression is now $2x^4 + 3xy$, choice **a.**

380. **c.** We distribute the $2x$:

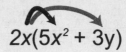

Note that $2x \cdot 5x^2 = 10x^3$, and $2x \cdot 3y = 6xy$. Thus, our expression is now $10x^3 + 6xy$, choice **c.**

381. **d.** On top, we can "pull out" a $3x$ from each of the terms in $3x^2 + 3x$. Thus, the top is equivalent to $3x(x + 1)$. We can pull a 3 out of the terms in the bottom: $3(x^2 + 4)$. Now, we have:

$$\frac{3x(x + 1)}{3(x^2 + 4)}$$

We can cross out the threes (3 divided by 3 is 1):

$$\frac{x(x + 1)}{(x^2 + 4)}$$

382. **b.** First, we'll distribute the square to all the terms inside the first set of parentheses. Remember that when raising a variable to a power, you *multiply* the exponents. When raising a number to a power, you just calculate its value as usual: Thus,

$$(3a^4b^5)^2(a^2b) = 9a^8b^{10} \cdot a^2b$$

When dealing with exponents, if you have the same base, and you are *multiplying* powers of that base, you *add* the exponents. Thus, $9a^8b^{10} \cdot a^2b = 9a^{10}b^{11}$.

383. **a.** We need to rearrange $PV = nRT$, such that we have T equal to something. We can easily do this by dividing both sides by nR. Thus, we get

$$T = \frac{PV}{nR}$$

384. **c.** Because we need an equation for V, we will first use $V = Er$. Now, the other 2 equations have $E = something$, so we can easily substitute them in for E in the $V = Er$ equation. But, because all of the choices have Q in them, we know we should use the $E = \frac{kQ}{r^2}$ equation. Thus, $V = Er$, becomes $V = \frac{kQ}{r^2} \cdot r$

Notice that we can factor out an r from on top and on the bottom. Thus, we get

$$V = \frac{kQ}{r^2} \cdot \not r$$
$$V = \frac{kQ}{r}$$

385. **d.** F only appears in Equation I: $E = F/q$. We can rearrange this equation to isolate F. Multiplying both sides by q yields $F = qE$. Now, because all of the choices have Q in them, we know that we should use the third equation,

$$E = \frac{kQ}{r^2}$$
Thus, $F = Eq = \frac{kQ}{r^2} \cdot q$

386. **b.** First we will isolate the x in the equation:

$$
\begin{array}{rcr}
5x + 15 & \geq & 10 \\
-15 & & -15 \\
\hline
5x & \geq & -5
\end{array}
$$

Next, divide both sides by 5

$$x \geq -1$$

387. **d.** We will isolate the x in the equation:

$$
\begin{array}{rcr}
2x + 37 & \geq & 63 \\
-37 & & -37 \\
\hline
2x & \geq & 26
\end{array}
$$

Next, divide both sides by 2

$$x \geq 13$$

388. **a.** We need to isolate the x term:

$$
\begin{array}{rcr}
5x - 27 & \leq & 43 \\
+27 & & +27 \\
\hline
5x & \leq & 70
\end{array}
$$

Dividing both sides by 5 yields:

$$x \leq 14$$

Thus, 13 is an acceptable value for x (choice **a**).

389. **c.** We divide both sides of the equation $5x < 23$ by 5 to yield $x < \frac{23}{5}$, and $\frac{23}{5}$ is equivalent to $4\frac{3}{5}$. Thus $x < 4\frac{3}{5}$.

390. **a.** First, cross-multiply to get: $B(D-A) = C+A$. Next, distribute the B: $BD - BA = C + A$. Now, we'll add BA to both sides: $BD = C + A + BA$. Next, subtract C from both sides: $BD - C = A + BA$. We can "pull out" an A from both terms on the left and make a set of parentheses: $BD - C = A(1 + B)$. And the last thing we need to do is to divide both sides by $(1+B)$ to get our answer:

$$\frac{BD - C}{1 + B} = A$$

SET 27

391. **a.** Combining all the p terms on the right, we get: $6p = 3p + 19 + 8$. Combining the numbers on the left, we have: $6p = 3p + 27$. Next, we subtract $3p$ from both sides to yield $3p = 27$. Finally, dividing both sides by 3, we get $p = 9$.

392. **b.** $1.25m + 7 = 17$ can be simplified by first subtracting 7 from both sides. This yields $1.25 m = 10$. Next, divide both sides by 1.25 to yield $m = 8$.

393. c. $12x + 2y = 80$, and we are putting in 6 for x, so we get: $12(6) + 2y = 80$. This equals $72 + 2y = 80$. Subtracting 72 from both sides gives us $2y = 8$. Finally, dividing both sides by 2 yields $y = 4$.

394. a.

$\frac{3x}{10} = \frac{15}{25}$ can first be reduced to

$\frac{3x}{10} = \frac{3}{5}$

Next, we cross-multiply to yield $5 \cdot 3x = 3 \cdot 10$, or $15x = 30$, and we can divide both sides by 15 to yield $x = 2$.

395. d. First, take $\frac{1}{4}x - 6 = 14$ and add 6 to both sides. The equation is now $\frac{1}{4}x = 20$. Now, multiply both sides by 4 to get $x = 80$.

396. a. A prime number is divisible by only itself and 1. Note, that by definition, 1 is not prime. Here, 47 is the only number that is prime. Its factors are 1 and 47. 51 is not prime. $3 \times 17 = 51$.

397. b. Just add 5 to both sides of $x - 5 = 31$ to yield $x = 36$.

398. d. $14x + 23 = 65$ can be simplified by first subtracting 23 from both sides, yielding $14x = 42$. Dividing both sides by 14, we get $x = 3$.

399. b. Cross-multiply to get $1 \cdot 63 = 9 \cdot x$, or $63 = 9x$. Next, divide both sides by 9 to yield $x = 7$.

400. c. First, combine the x terms on the left side to get $2x + 3 = 33 + x$. Next, subtract x from both sides to yield $x + 3 = 30$. Finally, subtract 3 from both sides to get $x = 30$.

401. c. First subtract 11 from both sides of $\frac{1}{5}x + 11 = 14$ to yield $\frac{1}{5}x = 3$. Next, multiply both sides by 5 to yield $x = 15$.

402. c. An easy way to get rid of all the fractions is to multiply the entire equation by 8: $8(\frac{x}{2} + \frac{x}{8} = 15) = 4x + x = 120$. Combining like terms, we have $5x = 120$. Divide both sides by 5 to get $x = 24$.

403. a. Use the formula:

$Average\ (mean) = \frac{sum\ of\ all\ values}{\#\ of\ values}$

Here, we know that the average is 81, and that there are 5 crates, so we have:

$81 = \frac{sum\ of\ all\ values}{5}$

Cross-multiplying, we get $5 \cdot 81 = sum\ of\ all\ values$, or $405 = sum\ of\ all\ values$. We know that the crates weigh 85 lbs., 70 lbs., 92 lbs., 105 lbs. and x lbs., so we set 405 equal to 85 lbs. + 70 lbs. + 92 lbs. + 105 lbs. + x lbs. Thus $405 = 352$ lbs. + x lbs., and $x = 53$ lbs.

404. a. Combining like terms, we get $5x + 4 = 7x + 13$. Subtracting $5x$ from both sides yields $4 = 2x + 13$. Subtracting 13 from both sides gives us $-9 = 2x$. Finally, dividing both sides by 2 yields $x = -4.5$.

405. d. We put -3 in for x in the equation $x^2 + x - 6$. Thus, we have $(-3)^2 + (-3) - 6$. This equals $9 - 3 - 6$, or 0.

SET 28

406. a. When we put 26 in for y in the equation $y = 3x - 13$, we get $26 = 3x - 13$. Next, we add 13 to both sides to get $39 = 3x$. Finally, divide both sides by 3 to get $x = 13$.

407. c. We insert 2 in for y in the equation $x = 13 - 4y$ to yield $x = 13 - 4(2)$, which means $x = 13 - 8 = 5$.

408. d. We put 37° in for C in the equation $K = C + 237$ to yield: $K = 37° + 273 = 310$.

409. b. $m = n(10 - 3) + (15 - n)$ becomes $m = 3(10–3) + (15–3) = 30 - 9 + 12 = 33$.

410. a. We substitute the values $a = 21$, $b = 2$, and $c = -3$ into the equation

$$\frac{2a - bc}{3}$$

to yield

$$\frac{2(21) - (2)(-3)}{3} =$$
$$\frac{42 - (-6)}{3} =$$
$$\frac{42 + 6}{3} =$$
$$\frac{48}{3} = 16$$

411. b. We put 5 in for z in the equation $y = 12z - (10 + z)$. This yields $y = 12(5) - (10 + 5) = 60 - (15) = 45$.

412. d. We're given $\frac{a}{(b - 1)} = 23$, and asked to find $\frac{3a}{(3b - 3)} + 7$. First, notice that in the denominator of $\frac{3a}{(3b - 3)}$, we can pull out a 3 as follows:

$$\frac{3a}{3(b - 1)}$$

Thus, the expression is now

$$\frac{3a}{3(b - 1)} + 7$$

We cancel out the threes to get:

$$\frac{\cancel{3}a}{\cancel{3}(b-1)} + 7 = \frac{a}{(b-1)} + 7$$

We were given $\frac{a}{(b-1)} = 23$, so $\frac{a}{(b-1)} + 7 = 23 + 7 = 30$.

413. b. Combining like terms, we get: $7y + 6x - 6y - 5x + 15 = y + x + 15$. We know $x + y = 5$, so $y + x + 15 = x + y + 15 = 5 + 15 = 20$.

414. c. The time difference is an hour and a half, or $1\frac{1}{2}$ hours. We use the formula $D = RT$, which stands for *distance = rate × time*. Here, we need to solve for **rate**, so we rearrange $D = RT$ by dividing both sides by T. This yields $R = D \div T$. Substituting, we get $R = 8 \div 1.5 = 5\frac{1}{3}$ mph.

415. a. We know together they fixed 55 computers, so $E + J = 55$. We also know that James fixed 5 less than $\frac{2}{3}$ of Erik's total, so $J = \frac{2}{3}E - 5$. So, instead of the J in $E + J = 55$, we put $(\frac{2}{3}E - 5)$. Thus, we have $E + (\frac{2}{3}E - 5) = 55$. Combining like terms, we get $1\frac{2}{3}E - 5 = 55$. We add 5 to both sides: $1\frac{2}{3}E = 60$. This is the same as $\frac{5}{3}E = 60$, so we divide both sides by $\frac{5}{3}$ to yield $E = 60 \div \frac{5}{3} = 60 \times \frac{3}{5} = \frac{180}{5} = 36$.

416. c. Use the formula $\frac{T}{5} = m$, substituting 15 for T. We get $\frac{15}{5} = m$; $m = 3$ miles.

417. d. Harry unloads 80 boxes in $\frac{1}{2}$ hour, so he can unload 160 boxes in 1 hour. How long will it take Keith to unload 160 boxes? We can set up a proportion:

$$\frac{120 \text{ boxes}}{1 \text{ hr.}} = \frac{160 \text{ boxes}}{x \text{ hr.}}$$

Cross-multiplying, we get $120x = 160$; $x = \frac{160}{120} = \frac{16}{12} = \frac{4}{3} = 1\frac{1}{3}$ hours. A third of an hour is $\frac{1}{3} \cdot 60$ min. $= 20$ minutes. Thus, it takes him $1\frac{1}{3}$ hours $= 1$ hr. 20 min.

418. c. If there is a 3:4 ratio of men to women, we can say that we have $3x$ men and $4x$ women. Notice how we preserved the ratio when we introduced the variable. We also know that the total number of people in the study group is $7x$ (because $3x + 4x = 7x$). So, $7x$ represents our total, which we are told is 21. Thus, $x = 3$. The number of men would then be $3x = 3 \cdot 3 = 9$.

419. d. Before the ratio was 5:1 (male:female). The total before was $T_{old} = 5x + 1x = 6x$. Note that $5x$ represents the number of men, $1x$ represents the number of women and $6x$ represents the "old" total. Now, after the 7 women joined, the ratio is 3:2. How do these 7 women affect our formula for the total? Well, no men joined so we still have $5x$, plus the old women and new women, which we can represent as $x + 7$, and the new total is then $6x + 7$. To summarize:

	Before (*old enrollment*)	After (*new enrollment*)	
5:1 ratio {	Men = $5x$	Men = $5x$ (*no men joined*)	} 3:2 ratio
	Women = $1x$	Women = $1x + 7$ (*7 new women joined*)	
	Total = $6x$	Total = $5x + 1x + 7$	
	Ratio = 5:1	Ratio = 3:2	

We can set the new 3:2 ratio equal to the algebraic values that we calculated:

$$\frac{3}{2} = \frac{5x}{x+7} = \frac{\text{men}}{\text{women}}$$

We cross multiply to get: $3 \cdot (x + 7) = 2 \cdot 5x$, which means $3(x + 7) = 10x$, or $3x + 21 = 10x$. We subtract $3x$ from both sides to yield $21 = 7x$, and $x = 3$. The question asks us for the current total, or $5x + 1x + 7$, which equals $5(3) + 1(3) + 7 = 15 + 3 + 7 = 25$.

420. c. Let's call the unknown amount of pounds x. We know that $(x \text{ lb.})(\$1.25 \text{ per lb.}) + (5 \text{ lb.})(\$8 \text{ per lb.}) = $ the number of pounds of the new mixture costing $5 per pound. The new number of pounds will be the original 5 lb. of nuts plus the x lb. of raisins, so we have: $(x \text{ lb.})(\$1.25 \text{ per lb.}) + (5 \text{ lb.})(\$8 \text{ per lb.}) = (5 + x \text{ lb.}) (\$5 \text{ per lb.})$. Notice how all our units make sense. Now we can ignore them:

$$(x)(1.25) + (5)(8) = (5 + x)(5)$$
$$1.25x + 40 = 5(5 + x)$$
$$1.25x + 40 = 25 + 5x$$
$$15 = 3.75x$$
$$x = 4$$

SET 29

421. c. Solve by using a *simultaneous equation*. The phrase *simultaneous equation* sounds intimidating, but it is actually an easy method for solving for one variable when you are given equations with two variables. You arrange your two equations on top of each other, and in this case, we add them together:

$$2x + y = 13$$
$$+ 5x - y = 1$$
$$\overline{7x \quad\quad = 14}$$
$$x \quad\quad = 2$$

Note that adding them together was a good choice, because we got rid of the y variables.

$$2x + y = 13$$
$$+ 5x - y = 1$$
$$\overline{7x \quad\quad = 14}$$
$$x \quad\quad = 2$$

422. a. Solve by using a *simultaneous equation*. You arrange your 2 equations on top of each other, and in this case, we subtract:

$$5x + 3y = 20$$
$$- (x - y = 4)$$
$$\overline{4x + 4y = 16}$$

Dividing the entire equation by 4 yields:

$$x + y = 4$$

423. c. Use FOIL to multiply the two quantities given:

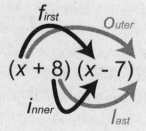

$$= x^2 - 7x + 8x - 56 = x^2 + x - 56.$$

424. b. Here we will use a simultaneous equation. Note that the question asks you to find y, so it would be nice to make a simultaneous equation that allows you to cross out x. The first given equation has a $3x$ in it. The second equation has an x in it. If we multiply the entire second equation by 3, we will be able to subtract it from the first and there will be no more x term! First, multiply $x - 2y = 4$ by 3 to get $3x - 6y = 12$. Next, let's line up our equations:

$$3x + y = 40$$
$$- (3x - 6y = 12)$$
$$7y = 28$$
$$y = 4$$

Note that we got "$7y$" because y minus a minus $6y = y$ plus $6y$.

$$3x + y = 40$$
$$\ominus (3x - 6y = 12)$$
$$7y = 28$$
$$y = 4$$

425. b. We are going to do a reverse FOIL on $x^2 + 12x - 13 = 0$, so we set up 2 sets of parentheses: $(x \pm ?)(x \pm ?)$. Because the coefficient on the x^2 term is 1, we know the missing numbers add to 12 (the coefficient on the x term is 12) and multiply to -13 (the *lone number* is -13). Thus, the numbers are 13 and -1. So, $x^2 + 12x - 13 = 0 = (x + 13)(x - 1)$. To solve, set $x + 13 = 0$ and $x - 1 = 0$. In the first case, $x = -13$, and in the latter, $x = 1$. Thus, choice **b** is correct.

426. a. First, let's make this equation look like the normal type of reverse FOIL question by moving the 24 over: $x^2 - 2x - 24 = 0$. Next, we set up 2 sets of parentheses: $(x \pm ?)(x \pm ?)$. Because the coefficient on the x^2 term is 1, we know the

missing numbers add to -2 (the coefficient on the x term is -2) and multiply to -24 (the *lone number* is -24). Thus, the numbers are 4 and -6. So, $x^2 - 2x - 24 = 0 = (x + 4)(x - 6)$. To solve, set $x + 4 = 0$ and $x - 6 = 0$. In the first case, $x = -4$, and in the latter, $x = 6$. Thus, choice **a** is correct.

427. b. The expression $2x^2 - x - 1 = 0$ can be factored into two sets of parentheses: $(2x \pm ?)(x \pm ?)$. Because the coefficient on the x^2 is not 1, focus your attention on the *lone number*, -1, which indicates that the numbers you will stick in the parentheses have a product of -1. The numbers will be a combination of -1 and 1. Because one set of parentheses has a $2x$, placement will matter and you have to just test out all combinations until one works. The working combination is $(2x + 1)(x - 1) = 0$. Next, you solve for x.

$$(2x + 1) \qquad (x - 1) \qquad = 0$$
$$2x + 1 = 0 \qquad x - 1 = 0$$
$$2x = -1 \qquad x = 1$$
$$x = -\tfrac{1}{2}$$

428. d. The fact that you see x^2 in every answer choice is a clue that FOIL needs to be used. So what goes in each set of parentheses? The first pair of parentheses will be filled by "five more than x," which is represented mathematically as $(x + 5)$. The second pair of parentheses will be filled by "1 more than twice x," which is simply $(2x + 1)$. The question asks you to calculate a product; thus we multiply using FOIL:

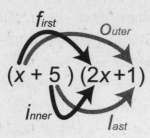

$= 2x^2 + x + 10x + 5$. This simplifies to $2x^2 + 11x + 5$.

429. **d.** "Five plus a number" can be expressed as $n + 5$. We multiply $(n + 5)$ by "3 less than the number," or $n - 3$. Thus, we have $(n + 5)(n - 3)$. Using FOIL, we get:

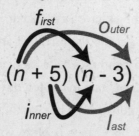

$= n^2 - 3n + 5n - 15$. This simplifies to $n^2 + 2n - 15$

430. **c.** Using FOIL on the left side of the equation yields: $10xy + 10x + 2y + 2 = 10xy + 12$. Note that you can cancel out a $10xy$ on each side. Now we have $10x + 2y + 2 = 12$. We subtract 2 from both sides to get $10x + 2y = 10$. Finally, divide the entire equation by 2 to yield $5x + y = 5$.

431. **b.** A *composite number* has more than two factors. Let's figure out an equation for the statement given in the question. "One more than the number N is multiplied by N" means $(N + 1) \times N$. Next, "is equal to 9 times N minus 12" means $9N - 12$. Distributing the N, we get $N^2 + N = 9N - 12$. Subtracting $9N$ from both sides, we get $N^2 - 8N = -12$. Next, we add 12 to both sides to get $N^2 - 8N + 12 = 0$. Thus,

$(N - 6)(N - 2) = 0$. It appears that $N = 6$ and 2. But be CAREFUL! N can't be 2, for 2 has only two positive factors (it is *prime*), so $N = 6$ only.

432. **b.**

$\frac{x - 3}{2x} \div \frac{x^2 - 9}{6x}$ is the same as $\frac{x - 3}{2x} \times \frac{6x}{x^2 - 9}$

$x^2 - 9 = (x - 3)(x + 3)$, so we get

$$\frac{x - 3}{2x} \times \frac{6x}{(x - 3)(x + 3)}$$

Notice that we can cancel:

$$\frac{\cancel{x - 3}}{2\cancel{x}} \times \frac{\overset{3}{\cancel{6x}}}{\cancel{(x - 3)}(x + 3)}$$

So, we have $\frac{3}{x + 3}$

433. **a.** $(x^2 - x - 6) \div (x - 3)$, is the same as $(x^2 - x - 6) \div \frac{(x - 3)}{1}$, or $(x^2 - x - 6) \times \frac{1}{(x - 3)}$

$x^2 - x - 6 = (x - 3)(x + 2)$, so the above equation equals

$$\frac{(x - 3)(x + 2)}{(x - 3)}$$

We cancel out the $(x - 3)$ in the numerator and denominator to yield $x + 2$.

SET 30

434. **b.** The numerator and denominator can be rewritten as follows:

$$\frac{x^2 + 9x + 14}{x^2 - 4} = \frac{(x + 7)(x + 2)}{(x + 2)(x - 2)}$$

Note that we can cross out an $(x + 2)$ in the numerator and deominator:

$$\frac{(x + 7)\cancel{(x + 2)}}{\cancel{(x + 2)}(x - 2)}$$

Thus, we have

$$\frac{x + 7}{x - 2}$$

435. a. The numerator and denominator can be rewritten as follows:

$$\frac{x^2 + 2x - 8}{x^2 - 16} = \frac{(x+4)(x-2)}{(x+4)(x-4)}$$

We can cancel:

$$\frac{(x+4)(x-2)}{(x+4)(x-4)}$$

Thus, we are left with $\frac{x-2}{x-4}$

436. b. The quotient of $x^2 + 4x + 4$ and $x + 2$ is expressed as

$$\frac{x^2 + 4x + 4}{x + 2}$$

The numerator can be rewritten as follows:

$$\frac{x^2 + 4x + 4}{x + 2} = \frac{(x+2)(x+2)}{x+2}$$

We can cancel:

$$\frac{(x+2)(x+2)}{x+2}$$

Thus, we are left with $x + 2$.

437. c. For this question, we need a constant rate formula: **distance = constant rate × time**, or $D = RT$. Drawing a diagram is a major asset:

The total distance between the 2 stations will equal the sum of the distances traveled by each train for the period of time in question.

$$\text{Total Distance} = D_A + D_B$$
$$210 = R_A T + R_B T$$
$$210 = (70)(t) + (50)(t)$$
$$210 = 120(t)$$
$$1.75 = t$$
$$t = 1\frac{3}{4} \text{ hr.} = 1 \text{ hr. } 45 \text{ min.}$$

438. c. We can apply the 3:2:1 ratio to an algebraic formula: $3x + 2x + 1x = $ Total Students. The $3x$ represents the math majors, the $2x$ represents the English majors, and the $1x$ represents the chemistry majors. We know that the total number of students = 12,000, so we have:

$$3x + 2x + 1x = 12{,}000$$
$$6x = 12{,}000$$
$$x = 2{,}000$$

Remember, we want English majors = $2x = 2 \times 2{,}000 = 4{,}000$.

439. a. 75 tickets purchased at $11.75 would cost 75(11.75). We would then add the 30 tickets at $6.75, which equals another 30(6.75). Thus, the total would be 75(11.75) + 30(6.75).

440. d. We use $D = RT$, and rearrange for T. Dividing both sides by T, we get $T = D \div R$. The total distance, $D = (x + y)$, and $R = 2$ mph. Thus, $T = D \div R$ becomes $T = (x + y) \div 2$.

441. c. We can divide the entire equation $5x - 5y = 60$ by 5 to yield $x - y = 12$.

442. b. Combining like terms, $4x + 8y + 2x - 2y = 48$ becomes $6x + 6y = 48$. We divide the entire equation by 6 to get $x + y = 8$.

SECTION 6—GEOMETRY

SET 31

443. d. The formula for the area of a square is: $A =$ (side)^2, of $A = s^2$. Here, the side is 12, so $A = 12^2 = 144$ square units.

444. c. The diameter goes entirely across the circle through the center. The radius is half the diameter. A radius is any segment drawn from the center of a circle to its edge. So if the diameter is 15 ft., the radius will be $\frac{1}{2}$ of 15, or 7.5 ft.

445. d. The designation *regular* hexagon means that all of the sides are equal. A hexagon has six sides, and when finding the perimeter we add up the distance around the hexagon: $4 + 4 + 4 + 4 + 4 + 4 = 24$ inches.

446. b. The diagram in the question has the diameter labeled as 12.. To solve for area, we need the radius, which is half the diameter, or 6:

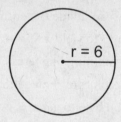

The formula for the area of a circle is $A = \pi r^2$, so we have $A = \pi(6)^2 = 36\pi$ square units.

447. c. *Adjacent* means "next to." Which angles are next to each other? Of the choices, the only adjacent angles are A and B, choice **c**.

448. a. The perimeter is the distance around something. For a square, you find the perimeter by adding up all of the sides. A height of 6 is given in the diagram, so the sides must be 6 as well.

Remember, a square has 4 equal sides, so all 4 sides measure 6 units each. Thus, $P = 6 + 6 + 6 + 6 = 24$ units.

449. b. Parallel lines are lines that, if extended onward forever in both directions, would never intersect (cross) each other. Most people think of railroad tracks when contemplating parallel lines. Trapezoids have 2 parallel sides and 2 non-parallel sides. In the figure $\overline{AB}$ and $\overline{CD}$ are parallel.

450. b. The formula for the area of a circle is $A = \pi r^2$. We know that $A = \pi r^2 = 25\pi$. This means that $r^2 = 25$, and $r = 5$. Circumference $= \pi d = 2\pi r$, so we have $C = 2\pi \cdot 5 = 10\pi$.

451. b. Perpendicular lines are positioned 90° relative to each other. We can tell that $\overline{BG}$ and $\overline{AC}$ are perpendicular to each other because there is a right angle indicated in the diagram. Right angles are 90°.

452. c. This question quizzes your knowledge of terminology. The following terms are presented:
- *Complementary*: two angles are complementary if they add to 90 degrees.
- *Right Angles*: Right angles are 90° angles.
- *Supplementary*: two angles are supplementary if they add to 180°. A straight line is 180°, so two angles that together form a straight line are thus supplementary.
- *Obtuse Angle*: Obtuse angles are greater than 90°.

Thus, by definition, angles a and b are supplementary. Choice **c** is correct.

453. b. The two triangles are similar. *Similar triangles* are in proportion with one another. When you have similar triangles you know that:
- All three corresponding angles in each triangle are equal.
- The corresponding sides are proportional to one another.

Comparing the big triangle to the smaller one, we see that its sides are *double* the small triangle's sides. $\overline{FG}$ must be double $\overline{BC}$, which is 4. Thus $\overline{FG} = 8$.

454. c. You can use the Pythagorean Theorem, $a^2 + b^2 = c^2$ to determine that the height is 8. ($6^2 + h^2 = 10^2$; $36 + h^2 = 100$; $h^2 = 64$, thus $h = 8$).

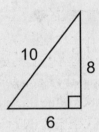

Then put the dimensions into the area formula: Area $= \frac{1}{2}bh = \frac{1}{2}(6)(8) = \frac{1}{2} \cdot 48 = 24$.

SET 32

455. d. Obtuse angles are greater than 90°. Only choice **d** is obtuse.

456. b. Hexagons have *six* sides. Two of the sides = 6, and the remaining four sides = 4. To find the distance around the hexagon, or the *perimeter*, we add: $6 + 6 + 4 + 4 + 4 + 4$.

457. a. Angle A forms a straight line (180°) with the right angle (90°), and is thus also a right angle (90°).

458. b. This question quizzes your knowledge of terminology. The following terms are presented:

- *Complementary*: two angles are complementary if they add to 90 degrees.
- *Supplementary*: two angles are supplementary if they add to 180°. A straight line is 180°, so 2 angles that together form a straight line are thus supplementary.
- *Congruent*: Equal
- *Obtuse Angle*: Obtuse angles are greater than 90°.
- *Isosceles Triangle*: An isosceles triangle has two equal (congruent) sides.

459. a. *Acute* angles are less than 90°. Only choice **a** is less than 90°.

460. c. Here, we need to calculate the perimeter, so we add up all of the sides: $48 + 48 + 23 + 23 = 142$ ft.

461. c. The markings on the polygon indicate which sides are equal to each other:

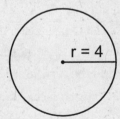

Thus, $P = 5 + 5 + 3 + 3 + 3 + 3 + 3 = 10 + 15 = 25$.

462. b. If $d = 8$, then the radius $= 4$:

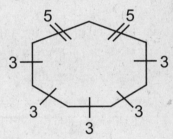

The formula for the area of a circle is $A = \pi r^2$, so we have $A = \pi(4)^2 = 16\pi$ square inches.

463. b. The area of a Circle B is $A_B = \pi r^2 = \pi(12)^2$ $= 144\pi$ square units. The area of a Circle A is $A_A = \pi r^2 = \pi(6)^2 = 36\pi$ square units. The difference is $A_B - A_A = 144\pi - 36\pi = 108\pi$.

464. c. A *regular* polygon has all sides equal. Only B, C, and E fit this description.

465. d. The rectangle's length = 8, and its width = $\frac{1}{2}(8)$. Thus, its area, $A = length \times width = 8 \times \frac{1}{2}(8)$.

466. a. We add up all the sides: $5 + 6 + 6 + 7 + 7$ $= 5 + 12 + 14 = 31$.

467. c. A straight line has 180°, and $91° + 65° + 24°$ $= 180°$.

468. c. *Complementary* angles add to 90°, so the angle complementary to 42° would be $90° - 42°$ $= 48°$.

SET 33

469. c. The area formula for a trapezoid is $A = \frac{1}{2}$ $(base_1 + base_2)(height) = \frac{1}{2}(4 + 5)(6) = \frac{1}{2} \cdot 9 \cdot$ $6 = 9 \cdot 3 = 27$ square units.

470. b. The area now is $A = length \times width = 14$ $\times 7 = 98$. If we double the width, the new width is 14, and the new area $= 14 \times 14 = 196$. 196 is *double* the original area of 98.

Old Area	New Area
$A_{old} = l \cdot w$	$A_{new} = l \cdot (2w)$
	$= 2(l \cdot w)$
	$= 2(A_{old})$

471. a. To find the surface area, you need to add up the areas of each face. 2 faces are 5×7, 2 faces are 4×7, and 2 faces are 4×5. So the surface area would be $2(5 \times 7) + 2(4 \times 7) + 2(4 \times 5)$ $= 2(35) + 2(28) + 2(20) = 70 + 56 + 40 =$ 166 cm^2.

472. b. Because all of the triangles are the same size, you can mentally rearrange the shaded regions to see that $\frac{1}{2}$ the square is shaded:

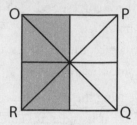

The area of the *entire* square $= (side)^2 = (7)^2$ $= 49$ square units. $\frac{1}{2}$ this area is shaded, so we take half of 49: $\frac{1}{2} \cdot 49 = 24.5$.

473. b. Notice the right triangle:

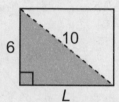

You can use the Pythagorean Theorem, $a^2 + b^2$ $= c^2$ to determine the length of L.

$$a^2 + b^2 = c^2$$
$$6^2 + L^2 = 10^2$$
$$36 + L^2 = 100$$
$$L^2 = 64$$
$$L = 8$$

474. a. Use the Pythagorean Theorem, $a^2 + b^2 = c^2$ to determine the hypotenuse (c).

$$a^2 + b^2 = c^2$$
$$24^2 + 10^2 = c^2$$
$$576 + 100 = c^2$$
$$676 = c^2$$

Note that $24^2 = 576$, so try to see what number squared would be 676.

$$c = 26$$

$P = 24 + 10 + 26 = 60.$

475. **c.** The area formula for a trapezoid is $A = \frac{1}{2}$ $(base_1 + base_2)(height) = \frac{1}{2}(10 + 12)(8) = \frac{1}{2} \cdot$ $22 \cdot 8 = 11 \cdot 8 = 88$ square units.

476. **d.** The old area is $A = (7)^2 = 49$. The new side is 2×7, or 14. Thus, the new area is $A = 14^2 = 196$. 196 is 14 *quadrupled* (times 4). Visually, you can see that the new area will be quadruple the old area.

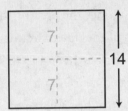

Old Area	New Area
$A_{old} = (side)^2$	$A_{new} = (2 \cdot side)^2$
	$= 2^2 \cdot (side)^2$
	$= 4(side)^2$
	$= 4(A_{old})$

477. **c.** The area of the entire square is: $A = side^2$ $= 4^2 = 16$ square units. Count to see that 10 out of 16 little boxes are shaded. This means that $\frac{10}{16}$ of the area of square HIJK is shaded. We take $\frac{10}{16}$ of $16 = \frac{10}{16} \cdot 16 = 10$ square units.

478. **d.** The question tells us that $\triangle ABC$ is similar to $\triangle XYZ$. The order in which they list the points of the triangle matters. Only the corresponding sides are proportional. Choices **a, b,** and **c** are all true. Only choice **d** is false.

479. **d.** The fact that all the answer choices have π in them should give you a hint that this question really deals with circles. A light shining 15 feet in all directions will create a circle with radius $= 15$. The area illuminated would then be $A = \pi r^2 = \pi(15)^2 = 225\pi$.

480. **c.** The triangles are not similar because their sides are not in proportion with one another. They also aren't congruent because they are not identical. So, this means that either choice **b** or choice **c** is correct. Here are the calculations for P and A for both these triangles:

Triangle A	Triangle B
$P = 4 + 5 + 3 = 12$ units	$P = 12 + 13 + 5 = 30$
$A = \frac{1}{2} \cdot 3 \cdot 4 = 6$ units^2	$A = \frac{1}{2} \cdot 5 \cdot 12 \cdot 30$ units^2

Thus, **c** is correct.

481. **a.** The total area to be covered is $4' \times 3' = 12$ ft^2. Each square foot would fit 9 tiles:

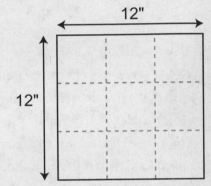

There are 12 square feet to be filled with 9 tiles per square foot $= 12 \times 9 = 108$ tiles total.

482. **c.** The greatest area for a 4-sided figure would occur when the 4-sided figure was a square. The perimeter, $P =$ side 1 + side 2 + side 3 + side 4. If all the sides were equal, a perimeter of 32 would correspond to 4 (sides) = 32. Thus, the side would be 8. A square with side = 8 has an area of $8^2 = 64$ yd^2.

483. **c.** A triangle is 180°. Therefore, the unlabelled angle must be 55°. (55° + 40° + 85° = 180°).

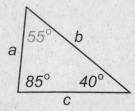

The longest side will be opposite the largest angle. Thus side *b* is the longest.

484. **b.** The distance around the circle would be $C = \pi d = \frac{22}{7} \cdot 14 = 2 \cdot 22 = 44$. The distance around the square would be $P = 4(side) = 4 \cdot 6 = 24$. Thus, the difference is $44 - 24 = 20$.

485. **b.** The area formula for a trapezoid is $A = \frac{1}{2}(base_1 + base_2)(height) = \frac{1}{2}(6 + 10)(4) = \frac{1}{2}(16)(4) = 8 \times 4 = 32$ square units.

486. **a.** All of the sides in $\triangle ABC$ are proportional to the sides in $\triangle DEF$. $\overline{AB}$ is 3 and $\overline{DE}$ is double that: 6. Thus, we see that there is a 1:2 ratio when comparing $\triangle ABC$ to $\triangle DEF$. This means that side $\overline{EF}$ will be twice $\overline{BC}$. Since $\overline{BC} = 6$, $\overline{EF}$ will be 12.

SET 34

487. **a.** Use the Pythagorean Theorem, $a^2 + b^2 = c^2$ to solve for the distance needed.

$$a^2 + b^2 = c^2$$
$$a^2 + 12^2 = 13^2$$
$$a^2 + 144 = 169$$
$$a^2 = 25$$
$$a = 5 \text{ feet}$$

488. **c.** The wedge that was moved represents $\frac{1}{6}$ of the area of the initial circular disc. We know this because of the angle labeled 60° (60° is $\frac{1}{6}$ of 360°). Thus, the piece that remains represents $\frac{5}{6}$ of the area of the initial disk. The initial area was $A = \pi r^2 = \pi(12)^2 = 144\pi$. $\frac{5}{6}$ of $144\pi = \frac{5}{6} \cdot 144\pi = 120\pi$.

489. **d.** The 9 feet by 15 feet area mentioned = 3 yd. × 5 yd., or 15 yd.². It costs 75¢ (or $.75) per yd.² to lacquer the wood, so it will cost .75 \$/yd.² × 15 yd.² = $11.25.

490. **d.** We need to find the area of the outer circle and subtract the area of the inner circle. The radius of the outer circle is 12. The area of the inner circle is $12 - 4 = 8$. The outer circle has an area equal to $A = \pi r^2 = \pi(12)^2 = 144\pi$. The inner circle has an area of $A = \pi r^2 = \pi(8)^2 = 64\pi$. Thus, the area of the shaded region is $144\pi - 64\pi = 80\pi$ ft².

491. **c.** The area of the entire square equals $A = (side)^2 = 8^2 = 64$ square units. $\frac{3}{4}$ of this area is shaded, so the shaded area equals $A = \frac{3}{4} \cdot 64 = 3 \cdot 16 = 48$ units squared.

492. **c.** The perimeter would be equal to $P = 64 = 2(width) + 2(length)$. We know that the "2 shortest sides of a rectangle add up to 24 feet," so the width must be 12. Thus, $64 = 2(width) + 2(length) = 2(12) + 2(length)$. So, $64 = 24 + 2(length)$, which means $40 = 2(length)$, and $length = 20$ feet.

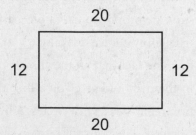

493. **b.** The area of the triangle is $\frac{1}{2}bh = \frac{1}{2} \cdot 14 \cdot 14 = 7 \cdot 14 = 98$ square units.

494. **a.** $\frac{1}{3}$ of the circle is shaded, so we need $\frac{1}{3} \cdot \pi r^2 = \frac{1}{3} \cdot \pi \cdot 6^2 = \frac{1}{3} \cdot \pi \cdot 36 = 12\pi$.

495. b. The formula for the area of a triangle equals $A = \frac{1}{2}bh$. Substituting the information presented in the question, we have $40 = \frac{1}{2}(8) \cdot h$, or $40 = 4h$. Dividing both sides by 4, we get $h = 10$.

496. a. The area of a trapezoid is $A = \frac{1}{2}(base_1 + base_2) \times h$. Here, a and b are the bases. We are given that the average of a and b equals 7, so we know $\frac{(a+b)}{2} = 7$. Notice that this is the first part of the Area formula. Thus, $A = 7 \times h$. We can use the diagram to see that the height is 5, so $A = 7 \times 5 = 35$ square units.

497. c. The sum of the angles inside a triangle equals 180°. Thus, we can label the third angle:

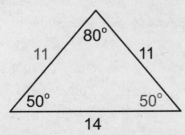

$80° + 50° + 50° = 180°$. Sides opposite equal angles are equal. Thus, the sides opposite both 50° angles are equal to 11 apiece. Now, we add up all of the sides to calculate the perimeter: $P = 11 + 11 + 14 = 36$.

498. d. The area formula for a square is $A = (side)^2$. Here, we know $4 = (side)^2$. Taking the square root of both sides, we get: side = 2. The radius of the inscribed circle is $\frac{1}{2}$ the size of the side of the square, and is thus 1. We need the area of half the circle, or $\frac{1}{2}\pi r^2$. Thus Area (shaded) $= \frac{1}{2}\pi(1)^2 = \frac{1}{2}\pi$ square units.

499. c. The area formula for a parallelogram is $A = bh$. Here, we use the Pythagorean Theorem to solve for the height:

Use the Pythagorean Theorem, $a^2 + b^2 = c^2$ to solve for the height

$$a^2 + b^2 = c^2$$
$$4^2 + h^2 = 5^2$$
$$16 + h^2 = 25$$
$$h^2 = 25$$
$$h = 5$$

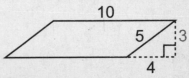

So, the area of the parallelogram $= bh = 10 \times 3 = 30$.

500. a. $P = 2(width) + 2(length)$. Because the length is twice the width, we put in $2w$ for length. Thus, $P = 2w + 2(2w) = 2w + 4w = 6w$. We are told that $P = 132$, so $6w = 132$, and $w = 22$. The length $= 2w = 2 \times 22 = 44$.

501. d. First, convert the 8″ into feet by multiplying by the conversion factor $\frac{1\text{ ft.}}{12\text{ in.}}$: 8 in. $\times \frac{1\text{ ft.}}{12\text{ in.}} = \frac{2}{3}$ ft. The volume of the container $= L \times W \times H = 3 \times 2 \times \frac{2}{3} = \frac{12}{3} = 4$ ft^3. When it is completely filled with water, there will be 4 ft.^{3} of water inside.

SET 35

502. c. Notice how the rectangle is divided into a 5-sided figure and a right triangle.

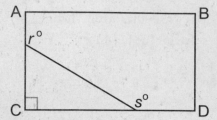

To calculate the number of degrees in a polygon with N sides you calculate $(N - 2) \times 180°$. The 5-sided figure then has $3 \times 180° = 540°$. There are 3 right angles, and $r° + s°$ comprising the 540°. We know: $90° + 90° + 90° + r° + s° = 540°$, so $270° + r° + s° = 540°$, and $r° + s° = 270°$.

503. b. The (x, y) coordinates of point B are $(-7, -2)$. From the origin $(0, 0)$ you go to the left 7 to reach -7. Then you go down 2 to reach -2.

504. c. Because the diagonal line creates corresponding angles for all the parallel lines that it crosses, we can fill in some more 50° angles in the diagram:

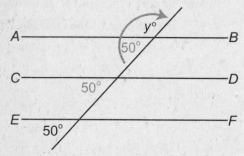

This newly labeled 50° angle at the top and the angle labeled $y°$ make a straight line. Because straight lines are 180°, we know that angle a must be 130° ($50° + 130° = 180°$).

505. b. Line II has *no slope*. *Slope* $= \frac{\Delta y}{\Delta x}$. No slope occurs when there is no change in x ($\Delta = 0$) because you cannot have a zero in the denominator. Here is the graph of Line II, as you can see $x = $ a constant value:

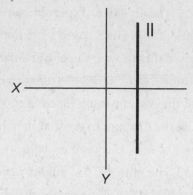

Note that Line I has a *negative slope*, Line III has a *positive slope*, and the slope of Line IV is zero.

506. a. The more hours she works, the more she earns. We need to find a plot that goes up as it goes to the right. This means **b** and **c** are wrong. Choice **a** shows a straight-line (linear) relationship, which would be appropriate for a plot of dollars per hour. Choice **d** is not appropriate because it curves upward in an exponential fashion.

507. b. The slope is calculated by using the formula $m = \frac{\Delta y}{\Delta x}$, where m is the slope of the line. We use the points $(-2, 4)$ and $(7, 3)$ in the slope formula:

$$m = \frac{\Delta y}{\Delta x} = \frac{y_2 - y_1}{x_2 - x_1}$$
$$= \frac{4 - 3}{-2 - 7}$$
$$= -\frac{1}{9}$$

508. c. The 50° and $n°$ form a straight line, so $n° = 130°$. Because $n°$ and $p°$ are *alternate interior* angles, $p = 130$.

509. **d.** Perpendicular lines have slopes that are *negative reciprocals* of each other. Remember, the *slope* is the *m* in the formula $y = mx + b$. The given line has a slope, *m*, equal to -2. First take the reciprocal of -2. $-2 = -\frac{2}{1}$. To take the reciprocal, we just reverse the numerator and denominator: $-\frac{1}{2}$. We also need to take the *negative* of this: $-(-\frac{1}{2}) = +\frac{1}{2}$. Only choice **d** has $m = \frac{1}{2}$.

510. **a.** We set the slope formula equal to 2:

$$m = \frac{\Delta y}{\Delta x} = \frac{y_2 - y_1}{x_2 - x_1}$$
$$2 = \frac{3 - q}{0 - (-3)}$$
$$2 = \frac{3 - q}{3}$$
$$6 = 3 - q$$
$$6 + q = 3$$
$$q = -3$$

511. **d.** First, notice that the 37° and the angle we labeled $w°$ below create a right angle. Thus, $w° = 53°$.

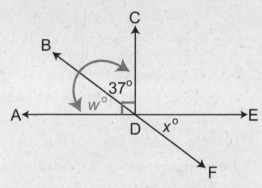

The angle labeled $x°$ and the angle labeled $w°$ are *vertical angles*, and are thus equal. So, $x = 53$.

512. **c.** The diagonal that crosses $\overline{AB}$ and $\overline{CD}$ generates corresponding angles. Thus, we can fill another x below:

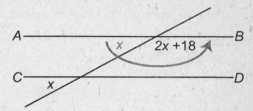

Notice that x and $2x + 18$ make a straight line, or 180°. Mathematically, we have:

$$x + 2x + 18 = 180$$
$$3x + 18 = 180$$
$$3x = 162$$
$$x = 54$$

513. **b.** The standard way to express the equation of a line is $y = mx + b$, where *m* is the slope of the line ($\frac{\Delta y}{\Delta x}$) and *b* is the *y* intercept. We rearrange the given equation $2x - y + 8 = 0$, to the equivalent equation: $y = 2x + 8$. This line will cross the *x*-axis when $y = 0$, so we set *y* equal to 0 in our equation:

$$y = 2x + 8 = 0$$
$$2x = -8$$
$$x = -4$$

So when $y = 0$, $x = -4$ and the (x, y) coordinates are $(-4, 0)$.

514. **b.** Parallel lines have slopes that are *equal*. Remember, the *slope* is the *m* in the formula $y = mx + b$. The given line has a slope, *m*, equal to 2. Choice **b** also has $m = 2$.

515. **d.** These lines will intersect when both their *y* values = 5. We set $y = x - 3$ equal to 5: $x - 3 = 5$, so $x = 8$. The point of intersection is $(8, 5)$.

516. **a.** The labeled angles are *alternate exterior angles*, and are thus equal. So, $3x = 2x + 36$, and $x = 36°$.

517. **d.** The sum of the degrees inside a triangle equals 180°.. So far, we have $51° + 37° = 88°$ accounted for. To find x, we subtract: $180° - 88° = 92°$.

SET 36

518. **b.** These two triangles are similar. We know this because they both have right angles, and they both have the vertical angles labeled below in common.

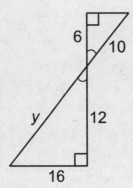

Therefore, the third angle in each triangle also must be equal. Similar triangles have all three angles in common and their sides are proportional. The 6 and the 12 are opposite the "third angle" in each triangle. Just as 12 is double 6, y (opposite the right angle) will be double 10, which is opposite the right angle in the smaller triangle. Therefore, $y = 2 × 10 = 20$.

519. **c.** First, the missing angle must be 60° because the angles inside the triangle have to add to 180°. Thus, we have an *equilateral triangle*. This means that all angles are 60°, and that all of the sides are equal.

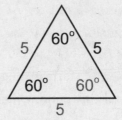

The perimeter would then be $P = 5 + 5 + 5 = 15$.

520. **d.** Remember that sides opposite *equal angles are equal*. Thus, both sides opposite the angles marked "x" are equal to 6:

$P = 6 + 6 + 5 = 17$.

521. **c.** As the wheel rolls, its outer edge is in contact with the ground. The distance around the outer edge is the *circumference*. A wheel with $r = 50$ cm. has a circumference $C = 2\pi r = 2 × 3.14 × 50 = 100 × 3.14 = 314$ cm. This means that for each revolution, it travels 314 cm. How many times does it revolve in order to travel 942 cm? $942 ÷ 314 = 3$ revolutions.

522. **a.** The volume for a cylinder is $V = \pi r^2 h$. The volume for a rectangular solid is $V = L × W × H$. The volumes for each of the figures are calculated below:
- Figure I: $V = \pi r^2 h = 3.14 \cdot (4)^2 \cdot 3 = 9.42 × 16 = 150.72$ units^3

- Figure II: $V = L \times W \times H = 3 \times 2 \times 1 = 6$ units^3
- Figure III: $V = L \times W \times H = 4 \times 1 \times 6 = 24$ units^3
- Figure IV: $V = \pi r^2 h = 3.14 \cdot (2)^2 \times 4 = 12.56 \times 4 = 50.24$ units^3

Thus, Figure I has the largest volume.

523. c. We know that the 130° angle and the angle right next to it form a straight line, so we can fill in 50° for that bottom angle. Also, if we think of this question as a "parallel line" question, we know that we can label an *alternate interior* angle at top. From there, we know that angles opposite equal sides are equal, so the other top angle is 50° as well:

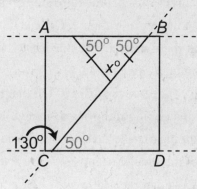

Finally, consider that tiny triangle at the top of the figure. We know that $50° + 50° + x° = 180°$, *so* $x° = 80°$.

524. d. If you quickly sketch the points, you can solve this by looking at the right triangle and using the Pythagorean Theorem:

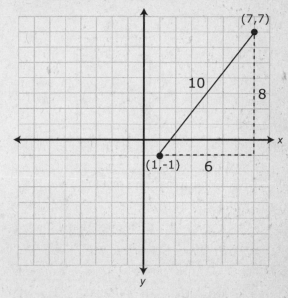

$6^2 + 8^2 = 10^2$. Thus, the distance is 10. Alternatively, you could use the distance formula: $d = \sqrt{(x_2 - x_1)^2 + (y_2 - y_1)^2}$. We get $d = \sqrt{(1 - 7)^2 + (-1 - 7)^2} = \sqrt{(-6)^2 + (-8)^2} = \sqrt{36 + 64} = \sqrt{100} = 10$.

525. d. We add up all of the sides: $x + x + 2 + 2x + x + 3 + 2x - 1 = 67$, or $7x + 4 = 67$, so $7x = 63$, and $x = 9$. Side $\overline{DE} = 2x - 1 = 2(9) - 1 = 17$.

526. b. We need to subtract the area of $\frac{1}{2}$ the circle from the rectangle. The width of the rectangle is 6 (given). The length of the rectangle is 3 + 3 (see below).

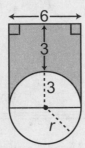

Thus, the area of the rectangle is $L \times W = 6 \times 6 = 36$. The area of $\frac{1}{2}$ the circle is $\frac{1}{2}\pi r^2 = \frac{1}{2}\pi(3)^2 = \frac{1}{2}\pi \times 9 = 4.5\pi$. The area of the shaded region is then $36 - 4.5\pi$.

527. a. We know $b = a + 2$, so we can replace $b - 3$ (the width) with $a + 2 - 3$, or $a - 1$. Area = $L \times W = (a + 2)(a - 1) = 28$. Using FOIL, we get: $a^2 + a - 2 = 28$, or $a^2 + a - 30 = 0$. This means that $(a + 6)(a - 5) = 0$, so a appears to be -6 and 5. However, it is impossible for a piece of paper to have a negative length and width! Therefore, the answer is $a = 5$ *only*.

528. b. First, add some dimensions to your diagram as you divide the deck into two rectangles:

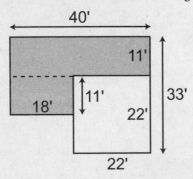

Now, we add up the areas of the two rectangles we created: $(11 \times 40) + (11 \times 18) = 440 + 198 = 638$ ft².

529. c. Note the dimensions of the label (when peeled from the can):

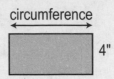

The area of the label will be $L \times W$ = circumference $\times$ 4″. $C = 2\pi r = 2 \cdot \frac{22}{7} \cdot 3.5 = 7 \cdot \frac{22}{7} = 22″$. Thus, the area = $22″ \times 4″ = 88$ in².

530. b. We put the given information into the area formula. $A = \frac{1}{2}bh$ becomes $28 = \frac{1}{2}b \cdot 8 = 4b$, so $b = 7$.

531. d. The third side of the triangle must be less than the sum of the other two sides (23 + 21) and greater than their difference (23 − 21). This means that the third side must be less than 44 and greater than 2. Only choice **d** does not fit these criteria. The side has to be *less than* 44, and *not equal to* 44.

532. b. The two triangles in the diagram are similar. Looking at the bases (4 and 8) we know that the big triangle has sides that are double the sides of the smaller triangle. We are given that $x = 6$, so we can replace $2x$ with 12:

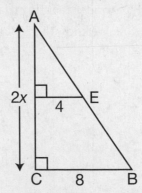

Note: AE = $\sqrt{52}$, half of AB.

We can solve for the hypotenuse, c, of the big triangle by using the Pythagorean Theorem:

$$a^2 + b^2 = c^2$$
$$12^2 + 8^2 = c^2$$
$$144 + 64 = c^2$$
$$208 = c^2$$
$$\sqrt{208} = c$$
$$\sqrt{4 \cdot 52} = c$$
$$2\sqrt{52} = c$$

SET 37

533. d. The volume of the cylindrical tank is $V = \pi r^2 h = 3.14 \times 3^2 \times 4 = 113.04$ ft³. Next, we know that every 7.5 gallons of water occupies 1 ft.³ of space, so we multiply the 113.04 by 7.5. Thus, we get: 113.04 ft.³ × 7.5 gal./ft.³ = 847.8 gallons.

534. a. The diagram shows $d = 20$, so $r = 10$. The area that needs to be covered is $\pi r^2 = 3.14 \times 10^2 = 3.14 \times 100 = 314$ ft². We divide 314 by $52\frac{1}{2}$ to find out how many bags are needed: $314 \div 52\frac{1}{3} = 6$ bags. Next, multiply by the cost of each bag: $6 \times \$7.50 = \$45$.

535. c. We were given a weight per cubic inch, so convert the height to inches. $h = 2$ ft. 4 in. $= 24$ in. $+ 4$ in. $= 28$ in. The volume of the cylinder is $\pi r^2 h = \frac{22}{7} \cdot 1^2 \cdot 28 = 22 \times 4 = 88$ in³. Next, we use the conversion factor $\frac{.25\,\text{lb.}}{1\,\text{in.}^3}$ to find out the weight: 88 in³ $\times \frac{.25\,\text{lb.}}{\text{in.}^3} = 22$ lb.

536. c. $V_{sphere} = \frac{4}{3}\pi r^3 = \frac{4}{3} \cdot \pi \cdot 4^3 = \frac{4}{3} \cdot \pi \cdot 64 = \frac{256}{3}\pi = 85\frac{1}{3}\pi$ units³.

537. a. First, find the height. Notice, that the height is a leg of a right triangle:

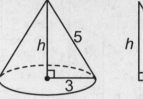

We can solve for the height by using the Pythagorean Theorem:

$$a^2 + b^2 = c^2$$
$$3^2 + h^2 = 5^2$$
$$9 + h^2 = 25$$
$$h^2 = 16$$
$$h = 4$$

Next, set $V_{cone} = \frac{1}{3}\pi r^2 h$ equal to $\frac{1}{3}\pi(3)^2(4) = \frac{1}{3}\pi(9)(4) = 3\pi \times 4 = 12\pi$.

538. a. $V_{pyramid} = \frac{1}{3}Bh$, where $B =$ the area of the base of the pyramid. The base $= L \times W = 3 \times 2 = 6$ cm². Next, we use the formula for volume: $V_{pyramid} = \frac{1}{3}Bh = \frac{1}{3} \cdot 6 \cdot 4 = 2 \cdot 4 = 8$ cm³.

539. c. Sketch out the circle:

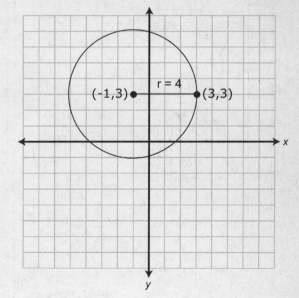

We see that $r = 4$, so $A = \pi r^2 = \pi \cdot 4^2 = 16\pi$.

540. b. Quickly draw yourself the circle:

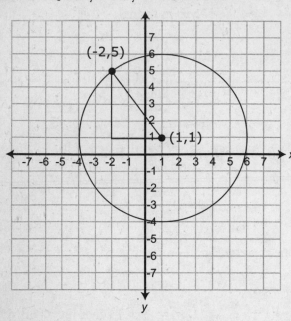

Notice, the 3-4-5 right triangle:

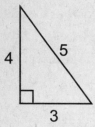

Thus, $r = 5$, so $d = 10$.

SET 38

541. c. Note that this is a 45°-45°-90° triangle:

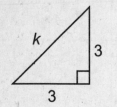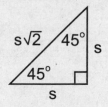

Thus, $s = 3$, and $k = s\sqrt{2}$, or $3\sqrt{2}$.

542. a. Here, we have a 30°-60°-90° triangle:

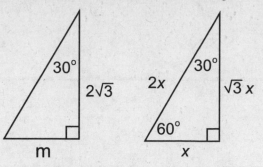

Note that $x = 2$. Thus, $m = x = 2$.

543. b. Notice the 30°-60°-90° triangle:

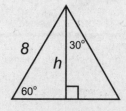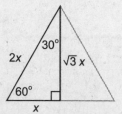

Note that $2x = 8$, so $x = 4$. The height corresponds with $\sqrt{3}x$, so $h = 4\sqrt{3}$.

544. b. Because both the legs of the right triangle are radii, we have a 45°-45°-90° triangle:

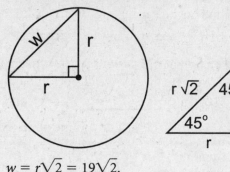

$w = r\sqrt{2} = 19\sqrt{2}$.

545. **c.** Notice that we have a 45°-45°-90° triangle inscribed in the circle:

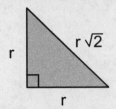

Thus, $P = r + r + r\sqrt{2} = 2r + r\sqrt{2}$. Compare this with the perimeter given in the question ($18 + 9\sqrt{2}$). Thus, $r = 9$. The area of the triangle is then $A = \frac{1}{2}bh = \frac{1}{2} \cdot 9 \cdot 9 = \frac{1}{2} \cdot 81 = 40\frac{1}{2}$.